Pilgrim
Without Boundaries

Ravi Ravindra

MORNING LIGHT PRESS

First paperback edition 2003
Published by Morning Light Press
323 North First, Suite 203
Sandpoint, ID   83864

www.morninglightpress.com

Printed in The United States of America

Library of Congress Catalog Card Number:
ISBN: 0-9740916-2-6

SAN: 255-3252

Other books by Ravi Ravindra include:

Heart without Measure: Work with Madame de Salzmann

Krishnamurti: Two Birds on One Tree

Whispers from the Other Shore: Spiritual Search East and West

Yoga and the Teachings of Krishna

Science and Spirit

Christ the Yogi: A Hindu Reflection on the Gospel of John

Science and the Sacred: Eternal Wisdom in a Changing World

Centered Self without Being Self-Centered: Remembering Krishnamurti

Contents

I am very grateful to Professor Anand Amaladass for inviting me to deliver the de Nobili Endowment Lectures at the Satya Nilayam Institute of Philosophy and Culture, Chennai/Madras in January, 2002. This book is is an expanded version of the monograph based on those lectures which was published as Satya Nilayam Endowment Lectures Series No. 5 in 2002.

Dr. Priscilla Murray has been of very great help in editing this monograph and bringing it to its present form.

—*Ravi Ravindra*

Hear my prayer, O Lord;
to my cry give ear;
to my weeping be not deaf!
For I am but a wayfarer before you,
a pilgrim like all my fathers.

—Psalm 40:13

charan vai madhu vindati

Wandering, one gathers honey.

—Aitareya Brahmana (7.15.5)

Have You a Pilgrim Soul?

Have you a pilgrim soul? Have you a soul that longs to glimpse the Mystery which keeps beckoning but which never wholly reveals itself? Are you a pilgrim in search of something—something which is not quite definable, though we may call it eternity?

Eternity—one can hardly utter the word without wonder, reflection, and inward silence. Whenever contemplation deepens and thought matures, what concerns serious people is eternity.

The closing pages of Herman Hesse's novel *Steppenwolf* include the following dialog:

> "Time and the world, money and power belong to the small people and the shallow people. To the rest, to the real men belongs nothing. Nothing but death."
>
> "Nothing else?"
>
> "Yes, eternity."
>
> "You mean a name, and fame with posterity?"
>
> "No, Steppenwolf, not fame. Has that any value? And do you think that all true and real men have been famous and known to posterity?"
>
> "No, of course not."
>
> "Then it isn't fame. Fame exists in that sense only for the schoolmasters. No, it isn't fame. It is what I call eternity. The pious call it the kingdom of God. I say to myself: all we who ask too much and have a dimension too many could not continue to live at all if there were not another air to breathe outside the air of this world, if there were not eternity at the back of time; and this is the kingdom of truth."

Eternity does not refer to an extension of time or to an everlasting continuation of time; it pertains to the timeless, to a dimension of being, of consciousness and perception, which is outside time. Everything that can be specified and defined belongs to the dimension of time and space. The laws of causality, which allow us to predict and control events, are all within the realm of time and do not apply to the eternal.

The eternal cannot be comprehended or possessed, though we may feel the need to seek it. It remains a mystery—not one which can be solved, but one which contains greater and greater depth, deeper and deeper truth.

> Men's curiosity searches past and future
> And clings to that dimension. But to apprehend
> The point of intersection of the timeless
> With time, is an occupation for the saint.
> No occupation either, but something given
> And taken, in a lifetime's death in love,
> Ardour and selflessness and self-surrender.
> For most of us, there is only the unattended
> Moment, the moment in and out of time,
> The distraction fit, lost in a shaft of sunlight,
> The wild thyme unseen, or the winter lightning
> Or the waterfall, or music heard so deeply
> That it is not heard at all, but you are the music
> While the music lasts. These are only hints and guesses,
> Hints followed by guesses; and the rest
> Is prayer, observance, discipline, thought and action.
>
> —T. S. Eliot, *Four Quartets*, "The Dry Salvages"

The major concern of wisdom, which is itself timeless, but which has been since ancient times, is the point of intersection of the timeless with time. It is not opposed to time or the things of time. As the Maitri Upanishad (6.15) succinctly says, "There are verily two forms of *Brahman* (the Vastness and the Real), *kala* (time) and *akala* (timelessness)." Wisdom is concerned with freedom from the hold of time, from the conditionings of the past and the imaginings of the future. In that state of being, one can act freely and freshly in time, and see that Nirvana is *kala-vimukta*. Nirvana is freedom from time, in time. Thus, wisdom, ancient or modern or future, acts in time to assist the transformation of anyone who wishes and is able and willing to pay the price, so that one can act in time while being anchored in eternity.

* * *

The blue god of the mysterious vastness, sometimes called Krishna, makes love to the pale Radha of time; and fecundates her with multiplicity and decorates her with wondrous ornaments!

A long time ago, and now, Krishna and Radha are living by a riverbank as householders. One day they received a message that the sage Durvasa, well-known for his austerities and short temper, is on the other bank with a thousand of his followers, demanding to be fed. As proper householders, Krishna and Radha undertake to do their part in the maintenance of order (*dharma*) by preparing food for the mendicants. When Radha is ready to carry the food across to the other shore, she sees the river in full spate and wonders how she can get across. Krishna says, "Go to the river and say, 'If Krishna is eternally celibate, O River, subside.'" Radha well knows the power of uttering the true word; but is this the true word? Of all people, she ought to know! She smiles to herself, goes to the river, and asks it to subside if Krishna is eternally celibate. The river subsides. She goes across and takes the food to the sage Durvasa, who is well pleased and eats heartily along with his disciples. When it is time for Radha to return, she again sees the river in full spate, and asks the sage for help. The sage says, "Go to the river and say, 'If Durvasa is eternally fasting, O River, subside.'" Radha had just seen the sage eat. She smiles to herself, goes to the river and asks it to subside if Durvasa is eternally fasting. The river subsides and Radha returns home to Krishna—where time and the eternal intersect.

The World is With Us, Always and Forever

We can see why the spiritual traditions, which are naturally concerned with wisdom, place so much emphasis on paying attention to the present moment, on being here and now. Now is the point of intersection of time and eternity. "If we take eternity to mean not infinite temporal duration but timelessness, then eternal life belongs to those who live in the present" (Wittgenstein, 6.4311). In practice, one sees the difficulty of staying in the present, the eternal now, in the face of the strong momentum of time. The greatest weapon Mara (the deadly tempter and obstructer) has, in his war against anyone wishing to wake up from the hypnotic sleep of fear and craving in which we all live, is time and temporal power. The enchanting imaginings which transport us away from the now and the real consist of dreams of the future and revisions of the past.

Cultural styles come and go; we accumulate more or less knowledge about this or that; we live a little longer or a little shorter. All this does not matter very much for the depth is in altogether a different dimension. To be sure, there are cultural styles, institutional forms, or varieties of education that can be more conducive to certain depths, whereas others are less conducive. But the quality of this insight, or the lack of comprehension about it, or the general societal conspiracy of evading it, are not essentially different today than they were in the days of the Buddha or the Christ, nor are they any different in America than in China. This fact is intimately connected with the well-nigh universal human condition: our occupation with the superficial aspects of ourselves and of our surroundings. By confining ourselves to this limited aspect of the whole, we acquire the impression that we are in control. This results in the assumption that we are the central agent in our lives. This soon leads to a self-occupation, which is really ego-occupation, the chief characteristic of the persistent dream about ourselves and about others. This is true for cultures as well as for individuals.

All social reforms seem to be essentially attempts to rearrange the contents of our dream by altering the social institutions that maintain a particular set of the conditions which shape larger or smaller cultural units. Different cultural units have different conditions, some more pleasant than others, but they remain at the same level. What is needed is a questioning of the notions which hold us, a questioning of the very state of dreaming, a questioning of ourselves in our entirety. We need to undertake a thorough investigation of ourselves, from the most superficial level, where each one of us is completely separate and distinct from the other, to the profoundest level in which we participate in the mystery that "all there is is Krishna" (Bhagavad Gita 7:18).

Such questioning is too radical for us to bear for any length of time—radical in the literal meaning of the word, namely what concerns the very roots: the roots of our existence, the roots of our being, and the roots of our possibilities. It is because we wish to escape the radical depths that we engage in arranging and rearranging the surfaces. Lest it should become clear to us how hollow we are, we undertake to reform others according to some ideology, or to convert them to some belief system or a new paradigm. It is much easier to begin to teach others than to realize in our core that at a very fundamental level we do not know and cannot know, as long as we are what we are.

The primary question is one of being rather than of knowing, of transformation rather than information, of freedom from oneself—from that part of oneself that is a participant in the social dream and therefore lives basically by the operating principles of society, namely reward and punishment, craving and fear.

The world and the times will sometimes be better and sometimes worse, but there is always change. Whether the time is short or long is not the important factor. What matters is how we are and from what depth we engage with the world. We live within the world of material objects and ideas, but we need constantly to be on guard that possessions and ideas do not imprison us. Wisdom consists, in part, in not building a psychological prison while building a physical house to live in. We need to remember that "every house is builded by some man; but he that built all things is God" (Hebrews 3:4). Real freedom and right internal order have to be continually regained, from now to now. They do not persist merely by a mechanical momentum from the past to the future, but they can be discovered again and again within the realm of time.

Those who seek the dimension not opposed to but different from that of time and achievement have a pilgrim soul. They seek to enter the dimension of eternity. Eternal life is not a life of endless duration, a time that lasts forever; it is a state of being in time, accompanied by the qualities of clear perception and love. The everlasting is not timeless. Anything that is everlasting is still in the dimension of time, whereas timelessness transcends this, for the category of time does not apply to it (Ravindra and Murray, "Is the Eternal Everlasting?").

To be a pilgrim is to be a searcher, a searcher for entry into the dimension of eternity. This cannot be known in the ways in which we know, it cannot be reached by the ways we have already understood. To set out on this journey, it is necessary to know that we do not know. This is not a celebration of ignorance, but a call for innocence, an openness to what is and a freedom from all that is known. This freedom is also a freedom from fear, for the simple reason that what is truly unknown can never be a source of fear. Fear is created by an imagined or expected loss of what we know. The unknown is a source of Mystery; the only feeling it can create is that of wonder. And fear and wonder cannot co-exist.

But this state of wonder is less frequently available than we wish; innocence is far too often, and far too much, sullied by cleverness and control-driven knowledge. It seems that we need to work at unknowing, to pay for owning nothing, and to make efforts to reach a state of effortlessness.

Make no mistake about this, if there is anyone among you who fancies himself wise—wise, I mean, by the standards of the passing age—he must become a fool to gain true wisdom. For the wisdom of this world is folly in God's sight. (I Corinthians 3:18 -19)

Pilgrimage—Journey of the Soul

You say I am repeating

Something I have said before. I shall say it again.

Shall I say it again? In order to arrive there,

To arrive where you are, to get from where you are not,

You must go by a way wherein there is no ecstasy.

In order to arrive at what you do not know

You must go by a way which is the way of ignorance.

In order to possess what you do not possess

You must go by the way of dispossession.

In order to arrive at what you are not

You must go through the way in which you are not.

And what you do not know is the only thing you know

And what you own is what you do not own

And where you are is where you are not.

—T.S. Eliot, *Four Quartets*, "East Coker"

We must start precisely from where we are, in the midst of our life, in the world, in this place, at this time. Our life is a symphony of which we are the conductors. The later notes and phrases are not going to be any more authentic or sacred than the ones we are now playing—unless we ourselves are transformed. Their quality will depend largely on what we

now try, and on what intention and awareness we now bring.
Our ordinary daily life is the very arena of our spiritual effort.

Spiritual practice involves the transformation of the
whole of ourselves—body, mind and heart. For this an
impartial self-knowledge is necessary, with all of one's
contradictions, fears and wishes. Daily life is the material
for a true self-knowledge. It is precisely where we live. Our
life is a hologram: any part of it contains the whole and can
reveal the whole. So, our gestures, postures, tone of voice, our
behaviour towards animals or the way we interact with our
neighbors—any of these is a fit subject for investigation and
can reveal a great deal about our inner selves.

Pilgrimage is the journey of our soul. In the Bhagavad Gita,
Krishna emphasizes the importance of *nishkama karma*
(desireless or selfless action). However, our usual life is
largely full of desires without purposive action (*nishkarma
kama*). The whole process of daily life as a spiritual practice
consists in the continuing transformation from the inattentive
state of *nishkarma kama* to a mindful state of *nishkama
karma*, the state when "the sage does nothing, but nothing
is left undone" (*Tao te Ching*). Thus ordinary daily life itself is
transformed, because the person who is living it is different.
We continue cooking, washing dishes, putting the garbage
out, lecturing, meeting friends, caring for our children, but all
of these acts then are fresh in each enactment. But mindfulness is not achieved or finished once for all; such a state
needs to be renewed again and again in each moment.

A Hasidic pupil was asked whether he visited his
master to hear his words of wisdom. "No," came the answer,
"I want to see how he ties his shoe laces" (quoted in Fromm,
p. 227). And when Krishna speaks to Arjuna about a person

of steady wisdom (*sthitaprajña*), Arjuna asks not what sort
of wonderful ideas such a person has or what his theology
or philosophy is, but "How does a person of steady wisdom,
who is established in *samadhi*, speak? How does he sit?
How does he walk?" (Bhagavad Gita 2:53-56).

Our daily life consists of walking, talking, sitting, tying
our shoe laces. The quality of these activities and of all our
relationships reveals and reflects our selves. It is an expression of our search for and our connection with mindfulness
and steady wisdom. We cannot disregard where we now are
and what we are now doing; we need to search for the real in
this very place and in these activities. As Krishnamurti said,

> The infinite is not **beyond** the finite, but it is **in** the
> finite. The eternal is not **beyond** the transient, but it is
> **in** the transient. The immortal is not **beyond** the mortal,
> but it is **in** the mortal. The immortal, the eternal and the
> infinite are thyself" (*The Little Book of Living*).

The eternal is to be found in time, right here, right now,
not over there, not later. There is nothing ordinary about
the events in our daily life, but an intensity of engagement
with those events is usually lacking. The three well-known
sights which Siddhartha Gautama, who became the Buddha,
saw—namely, an old person, a diseased person and a dead
body—are not so strange to most of us. There is hardly a
person who has not seen all of these three sights. But for us
it does not create the sort of psychological revolution it did
for the Buddha. For him these sights prompted a response
of total renunciation of life as he had lived it until then. He
set out in search of that which is not bound in the domain
of time where everything is, in principle, subject to change,
death and decay. He discovered that the way of freedom from

the tyranny of time is steadiness of attention, quiet mindfulness and constant vigilance.

> Vigilance is the abode of eternal life;
>   inattention is the abode of death.
> Those who are vigilant do not die;
>   the heedless are as if dead already.
>   —Dhammapada 21

The search in time for a state which is free of time is a
mystery. This is not a who-done-it kind of mystery which
can be solved by the discovery of additional data or of a
missing clue by smart sleuthing. This is a mystery not because
something is missing, but because it is overfull. It cannot be
solved but we can contact subtler levels of being—of body,
mind and heart—where it is dissolved. This mystery is like a
Zen koan. The solution is not a matter of having a published
solution of the koan, what is needed is a breakthrough of
consciousness which is naturally reflected in the way we talk,
stand or walk.

Daily life is not only the way but also the goal of spiritual
practice. We may understand something in a monastery or
in a cave or behind a tree, but we must return to where the
ordinary forces are at play and where we must have our
action for the sake of the world. Even after Arjuna has seen
the Great Form of the Godhead, a vision not vouchsafed to
many in the history of the universe, he needed to fight in the
battle as a warrior with force but without violence, for the
maintenance of the right order in the society.

Krishna said in the *Mahabharata* that the choice a person
faces is not between war and lack of war, or struggle and

lack of struggle. The only choice is always between struggle at one level or at another—a choice to be met again and again. We have to struggle in our world, in our daily life, against our own egos. If we are freed of our present level of existence, then we shall have to struggle at other levels. After all, even the angels or the devas have egos, and they too have to struggle.

Thus our ordinary daily life can become a true *sanyasa* (renunciation) not by renouncing the world, but by being free of worldliness. It is a form of dying to the world, which in effect is dying to one's old self. Then we can appreciate the profound saying of an ancient Sufi master: "If you die before you die, then you do not die when you die" which expresses the need for this freedom. The practice of dying is thus a practice leading to eternal life. St. Paul said simply, "I die daily" (1 Corinthians 15:31).

*   *   *

As many great traditions have said, we are a microcosmos mirroring the entire cosmos. Each one of us is in principle capable of having whatever possibilities and difficulties other human beings have—from the most exalted to the most degraded. The Buddha said that all the gods and all the demons are there within this very body. We do not always manifest all these traits, but nothing human is beyond us. The tourist, the archivist and the missionary lurk behind and inside every pilgrim soul. Pilgrims within us and around us are soon replaced by tourists, who wish to amuse themselves with new sights, and to collect souvenirs with photographs and anecdotes. Explorers are replaced by believers who convince themselves that they know and that they can start teaching others or converting them to the true faith that they have found. Searchers are replaced by researchers and archivists, who study cultures and religions, their own or those of other places and times.

But, the pilgrim soul is also there, wondering how to see with different eyes rather than how to see more and more things with the same eyes. The moment we specify the Vastness (*Brahman* in Sanskrit) as this or that, or cauterize the 'I AM' as 'I am this' or 'I am that', or make God look like Jesus Christ or Krishna or someone else of whom we have some material image, we are no longer pilgrims. In this, we may be believers or adherents of one faith or another, even strident missionaries; but not pilgrims. But the wish to come to the light and to see more and more subtly is also an urge of our souls.

Subtler levels in ourselves have a longing for the real which is veiled from us by the state of sleep in which we live. This longing may be activated by the words of great teachers, by scriptures, by stories of the journeys of other pilgrims.

There was a man, Moses by name, who had conversed with God as a man to a man, as the scripture says (Exodus 33: 11-23). He could not see the mysterious Glory of God, for no man saw this and lived. However for a few brief moments, the Mystery hid Moses from his own imperfections, placed him in a crevice in the rock and covered his eyes lest they should be blinded by excessive brightness, and Moses saw a hint of the Glory as it passed by. Ever since, the people who have followed the way of Moses, and such are always very few, for they have to walk in spite of trials, setbacks and despair, have nursed a pilgrim soul.

Hear my prayer, O Lord;

    to my cry give ear;

    to my weeping be not deaf!

For I am but a wayfarer before you,

    a pilgrim like all my fathers.

        —Psalm 40:13

Far away, in a different place and time, Arjuna had a pilgrim soul and longed to see Krishna's form in full glory, "brighter than a thousand suns". Krishna, who had been in one of his roles, Arjuna's friend and charioteer, said, "You cannot see my full form with your own eyes, Arjuna. I will give you divine eyes. Behold my magical power." Arjuna is joyous but afraid; he is completely bewildered and cannot bear it long. "Although my heart rejoices, my mind is troubled with fear... Resume your usual form Krishna" (Bhagavad Gita 11:8,11,45-46).

The difficulty comes because we search in time for what is eternal, we search with thought for what is beyond thought, we search for material proof of what is spiritual. We need to remain open to the whispers from the other shore, whispers of Mystery in the midst of this very life, in time, while engaged with things of time. We cannot capture this Mystery; by definition it cannot be comprehended, even by so great a man as Moses, though the Mystery, in all its glory, constantly reveals itself. There is no limitation in it; the limitation lies in the capacity of the vessel called to receive the entire ocean. Hence the need for transformation of our own eyes by divine sight.

A pilgrim soul is always at the threshold—wondering, hesitantly bold and impatient—preparing not only to understand truth but to withstand it.   What calls you, pilgrim? Things of time? Or the mysterious nothing of Eternity? Time does not comprehend Eternity, nor can the human soul of Radha encompass the God, Krishna, except when the eternal intersects with time, in a rapture of love, when Radha and Krishna are one.

Spiritual Quest

The struggle to know who I am, in truth and in spirit is the spiritual quest. The movement in myself from the mask to the face, from the personality to the person, from the performing actor to the ruler of the inner chamber, is the spiritual journey. To live, work, and suffer on this shore in faithfulness to the whispers from the other shore is spiritual life. To keep the flame of spiritual yearning alive is to be radically open to the present and to refuse to settle for comforting religious dogma, philosophic certainties, and social sanctions.

Who am I? Out of fear and out of desire, I betray myself. I am who I am not. I cover my face with many masks, and even become the masks. I am too busy performing who I think I am to know who I really am. I am afraid: I may be nothing other than what I appear to be. There may be no face behind the mask, so I decorate and protect my mask preferring a fanciful something over a real nothing.

I cling to the herd for comfort. Together we weave varied garments to cover our nakedness. We guard the secret of our nothingness with anxious agility lest we should be discovered.

Occasionally, I hear a voice uttered in some dark recess of myself. Sometimes it is the soft sobbing of a lonely child. At other times, it is the anguished cry of a witnessing conscience. At yet other times, it is the thundering command of a king. "Who are you?" I ask. I AM.

What am I asking when I ask 'Who am I?'? What sort of answer would be acceptable? Do I want a chart of my genealogical and social relations? A list of my racial and biological characteristics? A catalogue of my psychological features—my likes and dislikes, desires and fears? These are all the things that shape my personality. But whose personality is it? Who wears this mask? In response to a little knock at the door of my consciousness, I ask 'Who is it?' No naming is sufficient. What I seek is to see and touch the face of the one who calls.

'Who am I?' does not ask for an enumeration of scientific facts: it expresses a certain restlessness, groping, and exploration. It is the beginning of a movement towards light, towards seeing things clearly, as a whole. It is the refusal to remain in the dark—fragmented and on the surface of myself. It is a state of searching for meaning, comprehensiveness, and depth. It is the desire to wake up.

Soon I betray this impulse and am lulled back to sleep by comforting caresses and fairy tales. I sleep, dreaming of great adventures and of quests for hidden treasures. I dream of many journeys, many peaks, and of lions guarding the mountain passes. Sometimes for a moment I wake up to find myself a prisoner of what I know and what I am. Even finding the door of my little prison open, I stay in it, afraid to leave, counting and recounting my possessions and my testimonials.

> A bird in a cage
>> Its door wide open,
> With no practice in flying.
>> Sitting in the cage,
> Composing an ode
>> To freedom.

I share many walls with others. With vigor and imagination, I collaborate with others in building castles of science, art, philosophy, and religion in which we may rest secure, unmindful of our ignorance of who we are, why we are here, and why we do what we do. But the silent witness inside me asks 'What do you seek?'

The Human Condition

All spiritual traditions thus diagnose the human condition: we are asleep and our life, our ambitions, our fears, and our activities are governed by vast forces outside of our will or control. With instruction, grace, and effort, we can wake up, see our situation as it is, and begin to listen to our inner voice.

We discover the dream nature of our ordinary existence only when a shock momentarily wakes us up. When we come to, we realize we were sleeping; but soon the soporific forces lull us to sleep again. Most of our life is lived in dreaming—day-dreaming or wake-dreaming— and we see the world through a glass darkly: this is the Vedantist's experience of the thralldom of illusion or *maya*. It is only by lifting this veil of *maya* that one can become awake, *buddha*. If we open our eyes, we see that in our ordinary existence we are estranged from our real self and that we live in a fallen state. We are sinful because we have missed the mark; we experience suffering, dukkha, out of ignorance. We are not what we truly are; having forgotten ourselves, we have mistaken our identity.

When we begin to wake up, we realize the inner conflict between two poles of oneself: darkness and light, the lower self and the higher self (Plotinus), the little I (*ahamkara*) and the real I (*Atman*) of the Upanishads, the world and God (John), and flesh and Spirit (St. Paul). And this battle is waged in the psyche of human beings. The mind is the battleground of the Bhagavad Gita or as the Maitri Upanishad (6.34:11) says, "Mind, in truth, is the cause of bondage and of liberation." Upward and downward tendencies take hold of us periodically; in turn we affirm and deny our deeper selves. In this cosmic play of vast forces, we squirm like a fish on a hook.

The Ego

Central to spiritual life, both in the East and in the West, is the requirement to surrender the ego. Christ said, "If anyone wishes to be a follower of mine, he must leave self behind" (Matthew 16:24). This is essential. Beliefs, churches, rituals, or doctrines are not essential. The second birth is only possible after the displacement of the ego from the center of oneself. One of the main purposes of asceticism, esoteric traditions, and spiritual practices is to help us see the fact that by ourselves, as we are, we are nothing. Then we may be able to surrender the ego to the higher will and be reborn in the Spirit. "In my end is my beginning" (T.S. Eliot, *Four Quartets*) or as a Hasidic saying has it, "There is no room for God in one who is full of oneself."

What then is the ego? At the base of all our activities, there is some anxiety—physical, social, or metaphysical. Our minds are never quiet; constant scheming, calculating, and worrying produces the incoherent sounds of our internal talking machine. The roots of this universal anxiety are the desire to be something, to become somebody, to claim that I am somebody, and the accompanying fear of the failure of this claim. Corresponding to these, there are inner and outer postures and roles that we imagine for ourselves or we acquire from our conditioning. Then we identify ourselves by these roles. The constellation of these postures, pretensions, desires, fears—conflicting and changing—is the ego. Whatever in me hankers for acquisitions, possessions, and recognition, demanding my comfort, claiming my success, prestige, wealth and power, is my ego. We use a single word, but in reality, at the level of the ego, there is nothing permanent or constant, only confused and dispersed multiplicity—like a whole army of drunken monkeys in frenzied agitation, running helter-skelter without direction, aim or will.

All the actions of the ego are anxiety-ridden. Siddhartha the Buddha expressed it simply, as one of his four Noble Truths: the cause of sorrow, *dukkha*, is selfish craving, *tanha*. Our self-will, nourished by our craving, attempts to fashion the world according to our ego-interest. This absurd enterprise is bound to fail and our self-will suffers. It is this self-will, this ego, which we need to be free of in order to be prepared for another life. Indeed "nothing burneth in hell except self-will" (*Theologia Germanica*, chapter 34).

Self-will and self-interest dominate our lives and turn the world into a huge bazaar where we are all shouting at the top of our voices to attract attention and to make our little bargains. Christ said "my kingdom is not of this world" (John 18:36) for anything of this world, belonging to the web of ego, is opposed to the life of the Spirit. "Anyone who loves the world is a stranger to the Father's love" (James 4:4 and I John 2:15).

This is not to say that we should stop living in the world and commit suicide, or that we should somehow put up with the world until we die. Rather, it is a matter of basic orientation: it is not the world but our worldliness that opposes the Spirit. Christ prayed for his disciples, "I pray thee not to take them out of the world, but to keep them from the evil one" (John 17:15). It is the evil one who tempts us into selfishness. But in the life of a spiritual person, a sense of supra-worldliness pervades every act, transforming everything. When one is not driven by craving and is not under the sway of the world, one can operate under different laws, taking direction from inside. Then the most ordinary human activity becomes a sacrament and an act of worship. Action is then pure, simple, and in the present—without anxiety, which always concerns the past or future.

> A Zen monk asked his master, "In order to work in the Tao, is there a special way?
>
> The Master replied "Yes, there is one."
>
> "Which is it?"
>
> "When one is hungry, one eats: when one is tired, one sleeps."
>
> "That is what everybody does; is their way the same as yours?"
>
> "It is not the same."
>
> "Why not?"
>
> "When they eat they do not only eat, they weave all sorts of imaginings. When they sleep, they give rein to a thousand idle thoughts. That is why their way is not my way."

As we are, our ego-interest does not accord with the longing of our deeper self. We do not seek the inner kingdom above all else. In a reversal of the true order, we strive for the dominion of the world. If necessary, we even deny and sacrifice the higher for the lower, but "What will a man gain by winning the whole world, at the cost of his true self?" (Matthew 16:26). It is the false self, the ego, which is obsessed with winning the world. This ego is what we must overcome in order to be "born again ... of the Spirit" (John 3:7-8). Conquest of the ego is indeed victory over the artificial psychic world of our own making which we inhabit and which keeps us burdened and weighed down. Those who have overcome the world are from above and are not of this world; then, living in the world, these ones are not driven by worldly desires or ambitions. They do what is demanded of them from above, not for their personal satisfaction or glory.

The distinctive features of egoism are I-ness, isolated and separated from the rest of the universe, and my-ness, wanting everything for myself. These are the very core and substance of it and it is by these that one "binds oneself with the self like a bird in a snare" (Maitri Upanishad 3:2). These are the nuclei around which everything of the world revolves. A person of the world says: "I do this, I own that." Such a one is self-centered even when doing good works in the service of others. As long as any activity—praying, meditating, alms-giving—is controlled by our I, it is a selfish activity.

> This have I gained today, this whim I'll satisfy, this wealth is mine and much more too will be mine as time goes on. He was an enemy of mine, I've killed him, and many another too I'll kill. I'm master here. I take my pleasure as I will; I'm strong and happy and successful. I'm rich and of good family. Who else can match himself with me? I'll sacrifice and I'll give alms: why not? I'll have a marvelous time! So speak fools deluded in their ignorance. (Bhagavad Gita 16:13-15)

Selfless acts are done only by those who are not under the sway of their ego, who do not act by themselves or for their own self-advancement—on earth or in heaven. Those who are free of the hold of the ego respond to an inner demand which may or may not allow for their own convenience. "I do nothing of myself... I seek not mine own glory... I am not myself the source of the words I speak to you: it is the Father who dwells in me doing his own work" (John 8:28; 8:50; 14:10).

Thus there are two ways of acting: in the first, the self is the initiator, and in the other the self is an instrument which does the bidding of a higher will. The struggle between these two tendencies is the conflict between the profane and the sacred, our two natures. A great deal of confusion results from the fact that in either case—whether self is the author or a tool—language is used and acts are done by and through aspects of ourselves. We tend to consider only the immediate appearance and identify ourselves completely with the ego which usurps for itself the rights of authorship. Thus we live for ourselves alone, estranged from the person behind the mask of our personality. For us, as long as Self-realization is myself-realization; the demon of mine does not leave us.

What is usually called individualism is totally opposed, in its essence, to the spiritual point of view. The same is true of the modern, post-Renaissance humanism which regards the meaning and end of a given human life in terms of the individual and the fulfillment, glory or salvation of the particular person. Ultimately, from this point of view, the person is responsible to themselves, to their isolated, nuclear ego, sundered from the cosmos. Thus the individualistic modern person is vehemently self-centered, devoted to self-expression and self-fulfillment, acknowledging no higher authority. This is precisely the self which Christ said must be denied in order to follow him. One is, however, responsible for nourishing the deeper self within so that a true individuality can be expressed. This Self, however, cannot be controlled and manipulated by us. We may, in our stillness, allow it room; only then may we hear and obey It.

The Sanskrit word for ego is *ahamkara* which literally means "I am the doer." This word clearly expresses the egoistic point of view which according to the Bhagavad Gita (3:27-28) can be maintained only in ignorance: "Every action (*karma*) is really performed by *gunas* of *Prakriti* (forces of nature). One who is deluded by ego thinks 'I am the doer'. But those who have the true insight into the operations of the *gunas* and their various functions know that *gunas* act on *gunas*, and remain unattached to their actions." Everything that we see or sense, including our bodies and our psychic functions, are products of the play of forces of nature. The essence of egotism is for us to think that we are the maker of ourselves and of our destiny. Fooled by ignorance, we think we run the show, like the tribe whose members believe that the sun rises only because of their daily prayers. We are like kittens convinced that the doors open by the force of our mewing.

There is a Hasidic saying that the proud are reborn as bees, for in their heart the proud say, "I am a writer, I am a singer, I am a great one at studying." What is said of such people is true—that they will not turn to God, not even on the threshold of hell. Therefore, they are reborn after they die. They are born again as bees that hum and buzz, "I am, I am, I am" (Buber, p.103). This egotistic "I am" is entirely different from the "I AM" of the fullness of being uttered, for example, in Exodus 3:14 or by Christ at many places in John's Gospel.

According to a simile used in the Katha Upanishad (1.3:3-4), the human body is like a chariot whose steeds are the senses; mind or discursive intellect (*manas*), the reins; soul or contemplative intellect (*buddhi*), the charioteer; and the Self (*Atman*), the owner of the chariot. *Buddhi* is the integrated intelligence which stands between the human mind and the Spirit, between what is below and what is above, between the individual and the cosmos. It is useful to retain the Sanskrit word, *buddhi,* because any rendering into English is problematic, although the closest one word translation is 'soul' rather than 'mind' or 'Spirit' or 'Self'. *Buddhi* constitutes the subtlest and the highest faculty in human beings. It is above *manas* (mind, thinking faculty, ratiocination) and comprises the totality of human emotional and intellectual possibilities. It is the will that can orient a human being towards the light of the Spirit and give direction to the mind and the senses. On the other hand, if the senses get unruly, like the steeds of a chariot, they affect the mind, which in turn leads to dissipation and fragmentation of the *buddhi*. The *buddhi* has an amphibious character. It can dive into and stay in the lower world of matter, or it can soar into the higher realms of the Spirit. In the first case, a person is led into conflicting desires, illusion, and darkness— into sin, the cause of sorrow. In the other case, there is the possibility of movement towards light, towards understanding, integration, and unity.

Mind (*manas*) and the integrated intelligence (*buddhi*) both belong to our psyche and, along with our body, are the determinants of our individuality which, with effort and help, can serve a higher purpose. Belonging to our material nature, they represent our particularity—the specific collocation of forces and the peculiar combination that distinguishes each one of us from others. This is the field of individual deeds, memories, and thoughts; this is the realm of space, time, and causation; this is the arena of human efforts and knowledge. This is where we can purify ourselves, orient ourselves upward, and make ourselves available. One can attend to one's nets and lay them judiciously; then one must wait patiently, in readiness for what may come.

When one's lips have been cleansed with "a glowing coal," a call may be heard, "Whom shall I send? Who will go for me?" One may then, if one has the courage, become an instrument, a prophet, and say like Isaiah, "Here am I; send me" (Isaiah 6:6-9).

As we are, we are unable to see, hear, or understand higher reality, for we live in a state of self-preoccupation. If we recognize our situation, we can begin to be open to what is. We have to prepare ourselves to see and to hear—and to be there when we are called. We can do the divine will when we do not do our own. We have a right ordering within ourselves when we can say like St.Paul, "I live, yet no longer I, but Christ liveth in me" (Galatians 2:20).

Surrendering the Ego

Every spiritual tradition recognizes and attempts to reconcile a deep-seated duality in human nature. There is the lower self, the separated ego, enmeshed in the world, arrogating to itself the total identity of the person, in conflict with the Spirit. As long as we remain under its sway, we are "estranged from God" (Colossians 1: 21) and in sorrow. It is, however, possible for us to repent and come to our right mind, to reorient ourselves radically and to allow ourselves to be led by the Spirit. The Greek word *metanoia*, usually rendered as 'repentance' in the standard translations of the Gospels, is literally 'change of mind' implying a radical re-orientation.

But our assertive ego, supported by all the worldly forces, proclaims itself. Surrendering the ego begins to appear as suicidal and disastrous—contrary to our ideas about human development and success. We wish to deal with what is higher than us on our own terms. To us it seems that sages are beside themselves and not in their right minds for they behave as if they were dead to the world. But those who "possess the mind of Christ" feel that "the wisdom of this world is foolishness with God" (I Corinthians 2:16; 3:19). We have to be out of our worldly minds in order to be raised from the dead and made new in mind and spirit (Ephesians 4:22-24; 5:14). Only if we can leave our lower self behind, and be "crucified... to the world," can we be born in the Spirit (Galatians 6:14). As the Maitri Upanishad (6.34:6-7) says, "The mind, it is said, is of two kinds, pure and impure, impure from contact with desire and pure when freed from desire. By freeing mind from sloth and distraction and making it motionless, when one attains to the state of no-mindness, that is the last step." Clearly, the superconscious no-mindness being referred to here is not to be confused with a subconscious mindlessness.

When one is ended, is emptied out of self, one does not speak primarily as this or that person, with such-and-such a history. One does not speak then as a particular individual, for Self-realization is not self-expression. The Self is not yet another acquisition or achievement, however sublime. It cannot be won, coerced or violated. The Spirit is no more yours than mine; we cannot possess it. It is the Spirit that is the owner of the chariot. Leaves cannot lay claim to the wind. The Spirit is not personal and private; it is supra-individual and supra-cultural. Those who are born of the Spirit do not proclaim themselves, for, as Plotinus says of a transformed person, "this man has now become another and is neither himself nor his own"(*Enneads* 6.9.10).

All that socially or culturally defines these individuals is no longer of much significance. They have become non-entities from a worldly point of view, their kingdom is elsewhere. The Buddha is "neither priest nor prince nor husbandman nor any one at all. I wander in the world a veritable naught... useless to ask my kin" (Gottam Sn. 455-6). 2 Like Melchizedek, he "has no father, no mother, no lineage; his years have no beginning, his life no end. He is like the Son of God: he remains a priest for all time" (Hebrews 7:3).

The kind of knowledge that can lead us to the Spirit has a transforming character; in the process we become different. In order to know what is higher than us, we have to be higher. In fact, being and knowing are so intimately connected that the Mundaka Upanishad (3.2:9) declares, "One who knows *Brahman* (Absolute) becomes *Brahman*." For Parmenides (Diels, Fr. 185) and Plotinus (*Enneads* 6.9) "to be and to know are one and the same." Opening oneself to the Spirit is thus already a movement towards being born of the Spirit.

The liberated person, for whom the magical veil of *maya* is lifted, is no longer within the confines of space and time.

One who knows the Spirit, who has become the Spirit, is no longer any particular one, for such a person is identified with the very essence of the universal. The Spirit may, however, manifest itself through a given body and mind—through an individual in space-time—but that does not limit it. The ocean may give rise to waves and be active through them, but it is not limited by them. Our ordinary consciousness is only a small window through which we look at reality; from the point of view of higher consciousness, our vision is unnecessarily restricted. If we widen our doors of perception, we can see, not as we do now, but more clearly. One who is awakened to the Spirit dwells both in time and in eternity; although in time, one is not restricted by it. Eternity is not opposed to time, nor does it mean an infinite temporal duration, continuing on and on forever. No description exclusively in terms of time can be adequate for comprehending eternity, just as no combination of lines in two dimensions can produce a cube. In that sense, the eternal realm is timeless. We need another dimension of consciousness. As long as we remain confined to our ordinary consciousness, we experience and move only in time, having only vague and occasional hints of eternity.

In order to experience the timeless realm, it is not necessary to die physically; a reorientation of the ego is needed. In awakening, the tentacles of time and space fall away and we no longer live in the past or the future, but now, in the present, fully awake, radically open, time freed (*kalavimukta*).Then one does not live in the past or in the future, but now, in the present, fully awake, radically open. Eternity contains time within it just as a cube includes a square. A consciousness viewing our temporal world from an eternal and universal point of view cannot be limited by our notions of linear sequence of time and causality or of three-dimensional space. To it past and future events are as clearly comprehensible as the present ones; clearly visible are the objects far and near.

A person not confined by space-time becomes a seer and a hearer—one who sees and hears subtle things clearly. Whatever is eternal is always present, without beginning or end in time. "If we take eternity to mean not infinite temporal duration but timelessness, then eternal life belongs to those who live in the present" (Wittgenstein, Proposition 6.4311). Kierkegaard speaks of us being contemporaneous with the eternal, redemptive deeds of Jesus Christ and Meister Eckhart says of eternity. "Everything stands in a present now." The temporal order—past present and future—does not describe or delimit the eternal order. When one is liberated from time, one says with Aurobindo,

> I have become what before time I was
> A secret touch has quieted thought and sense:
> All things by the agent mind created pass
> Into a void and mute magnificence.
>   —"The Self's Infinity"

Sages are all agreed that Spirit is ineffable and beyond description. Just as It is neither red nor non-red, It is neither one nor many, neither plenitude nor void, neither in time nor out of it, neither within nor without, neither this nor that. It is neither nothing nor everything. All categories of thought and description derive their existence and meaning from It and not It from them. It is not defined or exhausted by any formula or symbol whatever. "By what should one know that by which all this is known? By what...should one know the knower?" (Brihadaranyaka Upanishad II. 4:14). Thought, knowledge, and language all function in time and can at best comprehend and describe what is temporal, not what is spiritual and therefore eternal. Negligence of this fact is responsible for innumerable doctrinal disputes in religions and for the problems which the philosophers pose. Like fools, we look at the finger which points to the far star and take hold of it as if it were the star.

In order to say anything at all about the distant star, sages have used various symbolic words, such as That, *Brahman*, God, YAHWEH, Allah, Suchness, Void, Absolute, Truth, Love, Nothing—all attempts to name the Nameless. So long as these remain only words, concepts and ideas, they are like dead coals without any flame. At their core, however, they embody the force of volcanic eruptions; they stand for the "devouring fire" which one approaches only with fear and trembling (Deuteronomy 4:24) in the sacrifice of the ego. One who experiences the baptism under fire may emerge melted down and reshaped, not as oneself, but as the very Person, as *Purusha*, as the Child of God. One may rise from the dead to "mature manhood, measured by nothing less than the full stature of Christ" (Ephesians 4:13).

What are we—we who are drawn by divinity and held down by our selfish concerns, we who hear the call from the other shore and betray it? The movement from this shore to the other is the spiritual pilgrimage. Our life touches both shores, but out of ignorance and fear we cling to this shore which we imagine we know and where we feel secure and in control. We do not know what will become of us and what we might do if we let go of our usual worldly props. Lest we make fools of ourselves, we choose to stay in the familiar prison of our little egos, trying to strike bargains with the unknown, using coins of piety, good works, and learning. But when we attend to the whispers which remind us of the other shore, when we remember that we do not know the purpose of our human life, when we yearn to be in touch with a subtler truth, we are reminded of the spiritual quest.

Religion as Living Experience

The spiritual quest and organized religion are related much like love and marriage: they can flourish together or separately. No doubt there can be feigning in matters of love, but counterfeit love does not last long because of the constant giving of oneself that is required. Marriage is another matter; people often marry for reasons other than love. It is a socially sanctioned arrangement which can linger on as a dead, dull habit. There have been awakened persons within religions, but also outside of them. Official creeds and theologies have sometimes helped spiritual search and sometimes hindered it; in general they seem indifferent to it. Often it appears as if their main concerns are primarily social and worldly.

One imagines that the only serious *raison d'être* of religious organizations, buildings, ceremonies, and doctrines is to help human beings in their struggle to lead a holy life, a life centered in the Spirit. However, the strength of worldly forces being what it is, in the religious sphere as in any other, means and ends often get confused. Not infrequently, institutions and officials find themselves unable to devote their energies to the sacred task of transforming "old" beings into "new." Old forms often become merely routine and repetitive. Worse still, what was made for the service of the sacred can be misused in the service of the profane—sometimes in the name of God and his prophets, sometimes out of ignorance, and sometimes out of willful misappropriation. To those innumerable officials, priests, and ministers throughout history, who traded in counterfeit spiritual wares for their own personal glory, safety or comfort, Jesus addressed these words:

> The scribes and Pharisees... preach, but do not practice. They bind heavy burdens, hard to bear, and lay them on men's shoulders; but they themselves will not move them with their finger. They do all their deeds to be seen by men...
>
> Woe to you, scribes and Pharisees, hypocrites! because you shut the kingdom of heaven against men; for you neither enter yourselves, nor allow those who would enter to go in. Woe to you, scribes and Pharisees, hypocrites! for you traverse sea and land to make a single proselyte, but when he becomes a proselyte, you make him twice as much a child of hell as yourselves.... Woe to you, scribes and Pharisees, hypocrites! for you cleanse the outside of the cup and of the plate, but inside they are full of extortion and rapacity. You blind Pharisee! first cleanse the inside of the cup and of the plate, that the outside also may be clean. Woe to you, scribes and Pharisees, hypocrites! for you are like whitewashed tombs, which outwardly appear beautiful, but within they are full of dead men's bones and all uncleanness. So you also outwardly appear righteous to men, but within you are full of hypocrisy and iniquity. Woe to you, scribes and Pharisees, hypocrites! for you build the tombs of the prophets and adorn the monuments of the righteous, saying, 'If we had lived in the days of our fathers, we would not have taken part with them in shedding the blood of the prophets.' (Matthew 23:2-30)

The spiritual effort is essentially towards awakening and rebirth. "Except a man be born again, he cannot see the kingdom of God" (John 3:3). In the necessary struggle of the individual with the soporific forces, organized religions have often aided the latter—sometimes unwittingly and with good intentions. Humanity seems to thrive on illusions. Most of us have neither the intention nor the internal resources required to make even the beginnings of an effort to rise from our common hypnotic sleep. What we seem to need, after bread and circuses, are solace, comfort, approval and the belief that a powerful, benevolent and forgiving eye has our affairs under its loving gaze. Any institution that would fulfill these needs prospers in the world. And religious institutions have become prosperous. Pundits and priests, if they suffer at all, are not necessarily suffering in the battleground of the Spirit. In spiritual matters, one sure sign of a counterfeit teaching is that it promises a great deal for very little effort on the aspirant's part: no genuine spiritual path is easy or comforting or self-advancing.

At their core, religions often carry whispers from the other shore; but these delicate sounds are drowned in the worldly din. Their adherents hang on to the words, bones, garments, footprints, and other fossils, reminiscent of a spiritual struggle and triumph. Religions are rooted in a search for truth, but they often settle for security and a comfortable pattern, a dead routine of litanies, rosaries, genuflection, benedictions and prayer-wheels. This is like hoping to paint a Rembrandt by numbers. Organized religions are by their very nature idolatrous—worshipping a person, a myth, an image, a place, or a concept. These are precisely what organized religions are organized around. Any of these worshipped objects may be of assistance and use in one's own search, but one has to be constantly on guard. Symbols can so easily shroud and then replace the very reality they are supposed to indicate. The finger that points to the moon can hide it if held too close to the eye.

Nietzsche's lament about a Christian being like everybody else can be equally well applied to the adherents of all other religions. The whole point of spiritual education is to bring about a change in the quality of a person's actions and relationships. It is not a matter of assenting to some doctrine, dogma, or formula—whether there is a soul or not, whether it transmigrates after death or not, whether the world was created at a definite time or not. As the Buddha said, "whether these views or their opposites are held, there is still rebirth, there is old age, there is death, and grief, lamentation, suffering, sorrow, and despair.... I have not spoken to these views because they are not conducive to extinction of craving, to tranquility, and Nirvana." (*Majjhima Nikaya*, Sutta 63)

Spiritual life is not ultimately a matter of belief in something, although this may be relevant at some stage of development. It is a matter of living—searching, struggling, overcoming. It is an effort to become what one ordinarily is not. And this transformation is not reserved for some special activities in some special places. Even the most ordinary act is done differently by one who is free. As was mentioned in an earlier chapter, there is an understanding in the Hasidic tradition, also echoed in Zen circles, that a pupil goes to a master not as much to hear a learned discourse, but to see how the master ties his shoe laces. No formula, however solemnly chanted, can by itself bring about understanding and change. "Not everyone that calls 'Christ' Lord, but he that does the will of the Father, shall enter the Kingdom of Heaven" (Matthew 7:21).

We read in the Vishnu Purana that those who give up their duties and simply proclaim the name of the Lord, "Krishna, Krishna", are verily the enemies of the Lord, for the Lord has taken birth for protecting righteousness. The great saint and poet Kabir says:

> Ages have passed turning the beads,
> But the turning of the heart has not occurred.
> Put aside the beads of the hand,
> And turn the beads of the heart.

A reorientation of the heart and the mind is called for, rather than scriptural learning, execution of liturgical detail or doctrinal dissertations. It is a movement in the new direction—away from selfishness and acquisitiveness—that imparts authority to the words of an awakened person. This authority is not ecclesiastical; it is moral and spiritual authority—from lived experience, not from hearsay or reading. Jesus Christ "taught them as one having authority, and not as the scribes." He spoke of what he knew, and testified to what he had seen (Matthew 7:29, John 3:11).

Theologians, philosophers, preachers use words, but not words of experience; mostly, they have no authority for they have not lifted up the curtain. They do not have the wisdom of the other shore; they merely run up and down this very shore, shouting slogans and trying to convert each other, too often in order to increase a sense of their own importance and security.

When a master's life and teachings are codified and formulated, we get at best only a photographic representation of a living person and the experiences which had been embodied. No amount of historical information or theological interpretation can add up to that blast of the Spirit that bloweth where it listeth, destroying and building (John 3:8). Literal truth, however faithfully recorded, remains flat unless vitalized by suffering and experience. The essential transmission of a teaching is not primarily a matter of preserving what the master actually said on any given occasion; it depends more on an inner understanding and assimilation by a few initiates in successive generations. Spiritual truth, more than any other truth, has this intensely experiential quality; unless it expresses itself in a person, even the greatest enunciation tends to degenerate into empty words and slogans. We can enlarge these words into more words by introducing finer and finer verbal distinctions; in the process we build an inner barrier between ourselves and our perceptions. The less touched one is by any genuine experience, the more one clings to words and rituals, and the more possessive and exclusive one becomes. But spiritual reality is comprehended only by those who do not want to possess it, who are willing to be naked and become vulnerable.

We can, however, start only from where we are. It is a part of the play of forces that we find ourselves where we are—under a given set of conditions and circumstances. The various cultural environments we live in give their own interpretation and colouration to the primordial search. These forms—philosophies, dogmas, rituals—are what we try to possess; and they are what we quarrel and kill for. All religions, like all philosophies, are ultimately lies; the very act of formalizing betrays the spontaneity of the experience. Is it for nothing that both the words 'tradition' and 'betrayal' are derived from the same root? At best the traditions present doctrinal and ritualistic interpretations of experienced reality. By themselves, without the presence of some searchers who are aflame with the fire of the Spirit, the traditions cannot perform the task of reintegration or making a connection with higher reality. The root meaning of both 'yoga' and 'religion' is 'to unite'. In an individual's effort to realign themselves with what is higher, it is indispensable that they work through themselves, for the self is the very stone out of which will be fashioned the sculpture of new being. In the process, the individual has to understand and overcome their cultural and religious conditioning. In the process, there are many aspects of the self which need to be let go. It is a process similar to the one Michelangelo described: "I saw an angel in the block of marble and I just chiseled and chiseled until I set him free."

Religions help to shape and mould our most basic attitudes and aspirations. This is true even for those who do not formally adhere to any religion, or would be loath to acknowledge any such influence. Religion is the most important factor in the formation of our cultural filters through which we perceive reality. According to the psychologist Carl Jung, "the religious point of view always expresses and formulates the essential psychological attitude and its specific prejudices, even in the case of people who have forgotten, or who have never heard of, their own religion" (Jung, p. 482). Those who would know themselves must know the peculiar covering of their societal religion, which protects them both from the darkness of moral chaos and from the glaring light of higher truth. When one is prepared, not only to understand truth but also to withstand it, one can set aside the protective covering and see. The great saint of the nineteenth century, Ramakrishna, was frustrated repeatedly by the image of his beloved mother goddess Kali, to whom he was extremely devoted, in his attempts to go beyond even her image and form in order to contemplate the Spirit directly: "Then with great determination I began to meditate as directed, and when this time also the blessed form of the Mother appeared before me, I used my discrimination as a sword and severed her form in two" (quoted by Swami Sardananda, pp. 319-20).

Divergence of Religions

In reality, of course, there are as many 'religions' as there are individuals—each one according to the background, need, understanding, and prejudice of the person. If we take the example of the most widely spread religion in the world and remember that there are more than two billion Christians at present and that there have been many more in the past two thousand years, we cannot but be struck by the immense variety within this religious tradition. The very erudite theologian St.Thomas Aquinas, a humble peasant, a village idiot, St. Francis of Assisi with overflowing love, the Inquisitors, and all manner of other people from a variety of types and levels have subscribed to Christianity in their own way. As William Blake said,

> The vision of Christ that thou dost see
> Is my vision's greatest enemy.
> Thine has a great hook nose like thine,
> Mine has a snub nose like to mine.
> —The Everlasting Gospel

Of course, there is an equally immense variety in other religions as well; we tend to imagine them as monolithic precisely because we are unaware of their internal diversity. Still, however different our individual religious understandings are, and however great the diversity is within each religious tradition, some grouping together is possible. Our spiritual sensibilities are conditioned by the society in which we grow up, the common language we use, and the traditions to which we are exposed.

If we consider two major streams of religious attitudes, referring to them in a short hand way as western and eastern, it would be reasonable to include Judaism and Christianity on one side and the two major world religions of Indian origin—Hinduism and Buddhism—on the other side. It is obvious that there are profound and irreconcilable differences between the two religions in each of the groups. However, these differences fade when we compare the two major streams with each other. Within the same group, there is a common heritage of sages and prophets and a shared soil of language and culture. There is a much smaller difference between the Christian God and the Jewish *Yahweh* than between either of these and the Hindu *Brahman*. And, in spite of much internal divergence, there are several ideas— for example, those of faith and uniqueness of history in the Judæo-Christian tradition, and of *karma* and reincarnation in the Hindu-Buddhist heritage—which are shared within the major groups.

In spite of the great variety within each tradition, we shall look at the clusters of ideas and concepts which are common in the western religious world-views and discuss them in relation to the clusters of ideas and concepts common in the eastern world-views to highlight the similarities within and the differences between the two major groups.

The Indian Tradition

The central call in the Indian tradition is that of *samadhi*, "the shining sun to which all Hindu religion points" (Prabhavananda, p. 67). Contrasted with the three ordinary states of consciousness—waking, dreaming, and dreamless sleep—is the indefinable state, *Turiya* (literally, 'the fourth').

The state of *samadhi* or *Turiya* is the accompaniment of Ultimate Freedom (*Moksha,* Nirvana). Mandukya Upanishad (7) says:

> *Turiya*, say the wise, is not subjective experience, nor objective experience, nor experience intermediate between these two, nor is it a negative condition which is neither consciousness nor unconsciousness. It is not the knowledge of the senses, nor is it relative knowledge, nor yet inferential knowledge. Beyond the senses, beyond the understanding, beyond all expression, is the Fourth. It is a pure unitary consciousness, wherein awareness of the world and of multiplicity is completely obliterated. It is ineffable peace. It is the supreme good. It is One without a second. It is the *Atman* (Self). Know it alone.

Much of Indian religious philosophy is a commentary on this passage. All Indian religions exhort human beings to strive for the "supreme good," knowing the Self. Notice that the supreme good for the sages in India has no reference to a God who is over and beyond human beings. *Turiya*, the highest state, may be ineffable but it is not beyond possible experience; it is transcendent only in the sense that it cannot be subsumed under any categories created by thought. But it is very much a part of us; ultimately, there is nothing superhuman about it. This state is unusual and extraordinary, like a monumental work of art but it is not beyond human beings.

The Upanishadic seers delved very deeply into themselves and experienced the *Atman*—imperishable, unchangeable, eternal. Externally, the nature gods of India had given rise to a monotheistic Deity, *Brahman,* (literally, 'the Great'), who stood above and beyond Brahma, Vishnu and Shiva (the Creator, the Sustainer and the Transformer). But now the seers had uncovered two Absolutes—*Atman* within, and the universal essence, *Brahman*, outside. Somewhere at the banks of the sacred Ganga was then uttered the exultant affirmation which has reverberated in the Himalayas ever since: the *Atman* that is within is identical with *Brahman* (Mandukya Upanishad 2). "Thou art That" (Chandogya Upanishad 6:8.7). The deepest essence of oneself is one with the essence of all other beings and of all there is. Ultimately, at the deepest level, there are no others. Otherness, separation of oneself from the rest of the cosmos, is a mark of shallowness. Only a superficial person, not the wise, thinks that one can live by oneself and for oneself, as distinct from the Whole.

The belief that even the gods are subject to natural laws is fundamental in Indian thinking and is responsible for the development of systematic steps of Yoga for realizing the unity of *Atman* and *Brahman*. It is precisely the same spirit which manifests again in the Buddhist belief in the chain of cause and effect. Also, this is the reason why there have not been major theological schisms in India over issues of salvation by works or by grace, as took place in the Christian tradition. Nothing can escape the law. There are indeed events which are mysterious and appear to us to be miraculous and supernatural. But these are not contrary to law; they are understood to be under different laws of which we may not be aware. These events are supernatural only in the sense of being supernormal, that is, uncommon, unusual and extraordinary. St. Augustine makes a useful distinction when he says that we must not regard wonders and signs as "contrary to nature", but only contrary to what is known of nature" (*de Civ. Dei*. Bk. xxi, ch. viii). Thus petitioning to God for something which calls for a suspension of the law is pointless. The only thing to do is to raise one's consciousness

so that one becomes aware of the higher-order laws and can
act accordingly.

The Vedic commands regarding the precise observance
of ritual, intonation and gesture in the sacrifices (*yajña*)
and the particular benefits to be derived from these were
impersonal, uniting the concepts of the unalterable law and
perfect omniscience. They imply, therefore, the possibility of
reaping all the comforts of this life and of the afterlife by
submission to these commands and compliance with them.
But they involve no lawgiver, no divine person, no author
of the universe or of the destinies of human beings, who
must be pacified, obeyed, or loved, and by whose grace we
receive the blessings of life. We can control our own destinies
and have whatever we want if only we follow the laws.
They represent an objective and unalterable law realistically
conceived. Vedic literature was considered as having existed
by itself from beginningless time, not created or composed
by any person, human or divine. The assumption of this
mysterious omnipotence of *yajña*, performed by following
the authoritative injunctions of the Vedas, forms the chief
trait of the mysticism of the Vedic type (Dasgupta, p. 9–18).

An inner and more esoteric understanding of *yajña*
thrived beside the exoteric and more literal understanding
of sacrifice. In the inner understanding of yajña, actual
sacrifices was replaced by the concepts of austerity and
effort. Regardless of the willingness of the gods, or even of
the nature of the performer, effort according to law was
rewarded. Indian mythology abounds with stories in which
a titan won some special power from one of the gods by his
own efforts—usually requiring superhuman strength and

perseverance which was then used to threaten the destruction of humanity.

According to the Indian notions of time and transmigration, every being—human, god, or demon—is immortal in the sense that individual existence continues endlessly in time, subject to successive births and deaths, forever. Therefore, what a spiritual aspirant seeks is beyond mere immortality (See Ravindra and Murray). The aim is an existence in a timeless realm where there is no birth nor death. When the titan, Hrinayakashipa, won the boon that he would not be killed by a god or by a human or by an animal, he was granted immortality in sense of continued existence in the same body and he started torturing humanity. The gods and humans were frightened and helpless in the presence of the terrible powers unleashed for destruction. According to the legend, the gods appealed to Vishnu, the Life Force, who is responsible for the maintenance of the cosmic order. Vishnu moved from his eternal repose and a great cry arose in all directions; then came the terrible silence in which every living creature held its breath, waiting. Even the all-powerful Vishnu could not break the law—the secret of immortality had been wrested by Hrinayakashipa with diligence and knowledge. The earth trembled and there emerged an awesome form of life—unprecedented, unforeseen, unimagined by humans, gods, and demons. Vishnu had incarnated himself as Narasinha—half human and half lion—a creature against whom the demon had not guarded himself. In the boon he had secured, he had protected himself not only against death at the hands of a known form of life but also against other pairs of opposites, such as above and below, day and night outside and inside. Vishnu went beyond the opposites and emerged from a pillar connecting above and below, at dusk, connecting day and night, and killed the demon on the threshold—neither outside nor inside, or both inside and outside. The law cannot be ignored, but a higher law can contain and override it.

Gradually, there was a further shift of emphasis on the kind of effort required by human beings to gain control over the natural forces—forces conceived as gods—whether for immediate material prosperity or for immortality. This shift was inward. With this shift, meditation and reflection replaced sacrificial rites and songs of praise. For example, the oldest Upanishad opens with an account of the horse sacrifice and interprets this as a meditative act in which the individual offers the whole universe in sacrifice in place of the horse; by renunciation of the world, spiritual autonomy is attained in place of earthly sovereignty (Brihadaranyaka Upanishad 1.1.1-2).

Parallel with this interiorization of effort was a reappraisal of the numerous deities, resulting in the conception of one Supreme Being. Thus, the Vedic religion shifted gradually from polytheism to what has been called henotheism which means that when one of the gods was worshipped he was called the Supreme God. The Vedic religion then slowly became monotheistic and then monistic, affirming the essential unity of all that exists.

In the Atharva Veda (10.7) we find a hymn dedicated to the god Skambha, in which the different parts of this deity are identified not only with the different parts of the material world but also with a number of moral qualities such as faith, austerity, fervor, truthfulness. All the thirty-three gods of the Vedas are contained within him and bow down to him. He is also called *Brahman*. This crystallization of the concept of the Absolute—the Being of all beings, the Essence of all essences—was the outcome of a great deal of effort in comprehending and systematizing the natural forces and the cosmic processes.

> Who knows truly? Who shall here declare, whence it has been produced, whence is this creation? By the creation of this universe the gods came afterwards; who then knows whence it has arisen?
>
> Whence this creation has arisen; whether he founded it or did not: he who in the highest heaven is its surveyor, he only knows, or else he knows not. (Rig Veda 10.129.6-7)

How can a human being to relate to *Brahman*, the Absolute? How can a person know It? Without this inquiry, *Brahman* would have remained only an intellectually derived metaphysical principle underlying a study of the external forces. The Upanishadic answer to the question 'What is the starting point in spiritual life?' is that it begins with oneself. Therefore, the basic spiritual question is 'Who am I?' This is where one must start in order to know *Brahman*. The Upanishads exhort us to know our true Self, *Atman*. That is the only way to know *Brahman*, for ultimately *Atman* is *Brahman*:

> One who knows that the individual soul, enjoyer of the fruits of action, is the *Atman*—ever present within, lord of time, past and future—casts out all fear. For this *Atman* is immortal... What is within us is also without. What is without is also within. One who sees difference between what is within and what is without goes evermore from death to death. (Katha Upanishad 2.1:5, 10)

Here is the fundamental turning point in the Indian tradition: *Brahman*, the One-without-a-second, is accessible, knowable through one's self. By uncovering the successive layers within oneself, one can come face to face with the kernel, the *Atman*. In the realization of the *Atman* lies liberation, *moksha*, and enlightenment, Nirvana—the goal of human life. To know the *Atman* is the supreme and unqualified good, the highest religion. This knowledge is not merely rational; to know the *Atman* is to have one's whole being transformed, for "one who knows *Brahman* becomes *Brahman*" (Mundaka Upanishad 3.2:9).

> To many it is not given to hear of the *Atman*. Many though they hear of It do not understand It. Wonderful is one who speaks of It. Intelligent is one who learns of It. Blessed is one who, taught by a good teacher, is able to understand It. The truth of the *Atman* cannot be fully understood when taught by an ignorant person, for opinions regarding it not founded in knowledge, vary one from another. Subtler than the subtlest is this *Atman*, and beyond all logic. Taught by a teacher who knows the *Atman* and *Brahman* as one, a person leaves vain theory behind and attains the truth...The *Atman* is not known through study of the scriptures, nor through subtlety of the intellect nor through much learning; but by one who longs for It. It is to be attained only by the one whom the *Atman* chooses. To such a one the *Atman* reveals its own nature... Like the sharp edge of a razor, the sages say, is the path. Narrow it is, and difficult to tread. (Katha Upanishad 1.2: 7-9; 1.2:23; 1.3:14)

The important thing is that, however difficult it may be, there is a path, a path which is different for each human being because the creative explorations of a person cannot be codified. Precisely because the goal, the truth, or *Brahman*, is beyond any form whatsoever, all forms of searching are to be respected. What is right and proper for me may not be at all suitable for you because you and I differ greatly from each other. The starting point for me is my own self; the path must be in keeping with my own individuality; the goal is the complete understanding of my innermost essence, the Atman. Religion is not a matter of assenting to some doctrine or belief but of striving to unveil the deepest layers of our being and making enduring contact with them.

Scholars have disagreed for millennia regarding the proper interpretation of the utterances of the Vedic sages. All the orthodox schools and perspectives of Indian philosophy accept the authority of the Vedas, which include the Samhitas (hymns), the Brahmans (ritual texts), the Aranyaks (forest treatises), and the Upanishads (philosophical discourses). But they hold different views regarding the nature of the *Atman* and the method of its realization. In some schools, the individual soul is related with the Supreme Spirit as children to a benevolent father who needs to be approached with devotion and self-surrender, much as in Christianity. In some other schools, there is no theistic conception of Deity as the Creator and Sustainer of the cosmos; in these, the spiritual essence of a person is said to be quite separate from the material nature, and the two are eternally self-existent.

The most influential school of thought in India has been that of Vedanta. The word 'Vedanta' means, literally, the end of the Vedas, with specific reference to the Upanishads, the last portion or the essential part of each of the four Vedas. The Upanishads make no attempt to order their contents but merely record the extraordinary experiences of the seers. In an attempt to systematize and interpret the Upanishads, Badarayana (500 BCE to 200 BCE) wrote the Vedanta Sutras.

From him we learn of other scholars who preceded him
in the same attempt but whose writings have not been
preserved. These sutras themselves are quite unintelligible
without commentaries. However, the Vedanta Sutras are
unquestionably of great authority, and every important
philosopher has written commentaries on them. The best
known of these philosophers are Shankara, the exponent of
an extreme non-dualism, *Advaita*, and Ramanuja, who held to
a qualified non-dualism. However, all of the Vedantic schools
are agreed that the ultimate goal is certainly the knowledge
of *Atman-Brahman*. The differences arise concerning the
methods for the realization of *Atman* and the interpretation
to be given to the ultimate state of liberation—whether
Atman becomes the same as *Brahman* or whether it
remains different in essence; whether devotion to Ishwara,
the personal God, can lead to final enlightenment or not and
other such questions.

The Buddha

In the vast spiritual and philosophical landscape of
ancient India stands the towering figure of Gautama Buddha,
the silent sage from the clan of Shakya, who radiates wisdom
and compassion. According to legend, he was born in the
6th century BCE in the north of India, near Nepal. Having
been forewarned that his son would be either the universal
emperor or a Buddha, the father of the future Buddha took
measures to keep him enthralled in the pleasures of the
world and unaware of the true human situation, but in vain.
The Buddha-to-be wearied of these evanescent pleasures
when he realized that all beings were faced with inevitable
decay, old age, and death. He renounced his possessions
and relations in order to seek the way for the cessation of

universal suffering. After studying with some of the best
known teachers in India, and practising austerities under the
guidance of some Brahmin ascetics, he abandoned intellectual inquiry and mortification in favor of the Middle Way. He
established himself under the Bodhi tree, determined not to
rise until enlightened. There he sat mindful and one-pointed,
in the centre of the cosmic spiritual struggle, meditating
without interruption until he became awakened, and
understood the nature of himself and of all other things, and
the causes of their appearing and disappearing. The Buddha
exulted in a song of victory:

> Seeking the building of the house
>
> I have run my course in the vortex
>
> Of countless births, never escaping the hobble (of death).
>
> All is repeated birth after birth!
>
> Householder, thou art seen!
>
> Never again shall thou build me a house
>
> All of thy rigging is broken,
>
> The peak of the roof is shattered:
>
> Its aggregations passed away,
>
> Mind has reached the destruction of cravings.
>
> —(Quoted in Coomaraswamy, p. 54n)

For the sake of other suffering beings, he then set in
motion the wheel of Dharma, the teaching leading to
enlightenment. At Sarnath (near Varanasi) he gave his first
sermon in which he spoke the Four Noble Truths and taught
the eight-fold path leading to nirvana and the extinction
of sorrow (*dukkha*). Although there are many points of
divergent emphasis between the Hindu and the Buddhist

traditions, particularly in their later developments, their differences on essential doctrines have sometimes been exaggerated. For the Buddha, just as in the Upanishads, "Self is the lord of the self" (Dhammapada 160). He advised his disciples to "take refuge in the Self" as he himself had done (*Samyutta-Nikaya* 111.143). In Buddhism, as in Hinduism, ignorance is the root of all evil and suffering. In Hinduism the ignorance is of who we are; in Buddhism of who we are not. In either case, it is only by right knowledge that human beings can be delivered of this evil and attain Nirvana.

Liberation from Within

In spite of the greatly divergent metaphysical views held by the various scholars and sages, the entire Indian tradition is agreed on one thing: liberation is within oneself and consists in the attainment of the true status of the individual. Belief and conduct, rites and ceremonies, authorities and dogma, are assigned a place subordinate to the art of conscious self-discovery. To know the *Atman* is the only goal. This *Atman* is beyond words and beyond rituals. "Considering religion to be observance of rituals and performance of acts of charity, the deluded remain ignorant of the highest good," says Mundaka Upanishad (1.2:10). Even scripture ceases to be authoritative when the awakening takes place. These rituals, scriptures, and images can all be helpful in a person's spiritual development, but after a certain stage they may become impediments. Whenever the symbols tend to obscure and supersede the real, the symbols, however precious and dear, must be discarded. Ramakrishna tells us:

> After the initiation, the naked one [Tota Puri, his teacher] asked me to withdraw my mind from all objects and to

become absorbed in contemplation of the *Atman*. But
as soon as I withdrew my mind from the external world,
the familiar form of the blissful Mother [Goddess Kali, of
whom he was a devotee] radiant and of the essence of
pure consciousness, appeared before me as a living
reality and I said to the naked one, "It is hopeless. I
cannot raise my mind to the unconditioned state and
reach the *Atman*." He grew excited and sharply said,
"What! You say you can't do it! No, you must!" So saying
he looked about him, and finding a piece of broken glass
picked it up. Pressing its point between my eyebrows,
he said, "Concentrate the mind on this point." Then with
great determination I began to meditate as directed,
and when this time also the blessed form of the Mother
appeared before me, I used my discrimination as a sword
and severed her form in two. Then my mind soared
immediately beyond all duality and entered into
nirvikalpa, the non-dual, unitary consciousness.
(Sardananda, pp. 319 – 20)

Ultimately, the concern is not with any specific doctrine,
church, or belief. The problem is one of consciousness and
transcendental experience. The seers have experienced an
order of reality which is more basic and transforming. They
exhort everyone to discover this reality in themselves.

Vivekananda, one of the modern sages of India, says:

Do not depend on doctrines, do not depend on dogmas
or sects, or churches, or temples: they count for little
compared with the essence of existence in man, which
is divine; and the more this divinity is developed in a
man, the more powerful is he for good. Show by your
lives that religion does not mean words, or names, or
sects, but that it means spiritual realization. (pp.182-3)

It is an exacting command which the Buddha taught, "not
a doctrine for the sluggard but for the person who puts forth
virile effort" (*Anguttara-Nikaya* IV). It does not offer

peace and security, it insists on personal responsibility and freedom—from the world as well as from God. The Buddha said (*Mahaparinibbana Sutta* 11.33), "Be a refuge to yourselves. Betake yourselves to no external refuge."

The Judæo-Christian Tradition

> I will lift up mine eyes unto the hills,
>> from whence cometh my help.
> My help cometh from the Lord,
>> which made heaven and earth.
> He will not suffer thy foot to be moved:
> He that keepeth thee will not slumber.
> Behold, he that keepeth Israel
>> shall neither slumber nor sleep.
> The Lord is thy keeper: the Lord is thy
>> shade upon thy right hand.
> The sun shall not smite thee by day,
>> nor the moon by night.
> The Lord shall preserve thee from all evil:
> He shall preserve thy soul.
> The Lord shall preserve thy going out and
>> thy coming in from this time forth,
>> and even for evermore. (Psalm 121)

This psalm beautifully sings the Judæo-Christian faith and hope in one single God who is all-powerful, eternally awake, and full of mercy. "Hear O Israel," says the Jewish Shema, "the Lord our God, the Lord is one." He is Omnipresent, Omnipotent, and Omniscient; to Him belongs all power and glory. He is compassionate and just. "Whoever does something wrong and repents of it he is forgiven at once" (Hagiga 5a and Sanhedrin 38b; cited in Fromm, p. 172). Fromm also points out that the rabbinic view has interpreted YHWH as denoting God under His attribute of compassion; Elohim under the attribute of justice. The idea of God's forgiveness is also expressed in the view that God has two thrones: one for justice and another for compassion. There is surely justice and the wrongdoers will be punished, but God will show mercy to the contrite heart.

All the Biblical religions—Judaism, Christianity, and Islam—accept the view that the first fundamental revelation of God to human beings was His revelation of the truth of monotheism to Abraham. "I am the Almighty God, walk before me, and be thou perfect. And I will make my covenant between me and thee, and will multiply thee exceedingly... I am thy shield, and thy exceeding great reward" (Genesis 17:1-2; 15:1). Already in his dealings with Abraham, God had revealed Himself as One who brings His people forth, and leads them and guides them. The prophets from Moses to Jeremiah recognized him afterwards in this way. Here, as Buber remarks, "we have nothing to do with the 'projection' of later prophetic experience, but rather with its simple early beginning. The bringing forth belongs to the nature of this God as well as [His] leading"(Buber, 1962, pp.35-36).

God sealed the covenant which He made with the giving of a new name, Abraham, to Abram. The giving of a new name in the Bible always signifies a momentous event and marks a radical change in being of the person receiving the new name. In this case, it was a mark of having been chosen by God. The God who goes forth with these people goes with

His chosen people, who also chose Him. He separates these people from others who are not chosen, and keeps them in His presence, as He is going with them. In the innumerable vicissitudes in the history of Israel, to quote Buber again, "this combination, this 'correlation' of guidance and devotion, revelation and decision, God's love for man and man's love for God, this unconditional relation between Him and men remains" (Buber, 1960, p. 36).

The relationship between a human being and God is between a person and the Person—it is entirely personal. That is not to say that this relationship is subjective, in the sense of being arbitrary, wishful, egoistic, or idiosyncratic. It is an objective relationship between the very essence of a person, the soul, and God, the Highest Person. This God is far from an impersonal principle; He is the Living God who enters into dialogue with His chosen people, who shields them and leads them personally, through His prophets (The Greek word '*prophetes*' means 'to speak for', 'to be an instrument of) who speak on His authority because He has revealed Himself to them and commanded them to do so. As the prophet Jeremiah said, "Then the Lord put forth His hand, and touched my mouth. And the Lord said unto me, 'Behold, I have put my words in thy mouth'" (Jeremiah 1: 9). All the Biblical prophets—from Abraham through Moses and Jesus to Mohammed—speak on His authority and do His bidding, often unwillingly. The Terrible One seizes them and commands them to go forth in His name, and they obey. Their strength lies in the submission of their wills to the Will of God who rules over human history and intervenes in it when necessary.

God's Community

The angel of the Lord said to Jacob, "Thy name shall be called no more Jacob, but Israel; for as a prince hast thou power with God and with men, and hast prevailed" (Genesis 32:28). Innumerable times after this, Yahweh, described in Exodus (3:14) as 'I AM' is called the Lord, God of Israel. The name Israel no longer refers to one Patriarch but to "His People." God of Israel is the God of a community—the chosen people. Even Jesus acknowledges this: "I am not sent," said Jesus, "but unto the lost sheep of the house of Israel" (Matthew 15:24). It is not known whether Israel was originally the name of a people or the name of a holy confederacy to which the tribes were gathered together by the leadership of Moses. In either case, the name 'Israel' means either "striven with God" or "God rules."

Whatever the historical origin of the name of the community may be, it is clear from the scriptures that the revelations of God—including His revelation as Jesus Christ as recorded in the New Testament—were not a private matter between God and one person. God did not reveal Himself for the salvation of one individual soul, however exalted that one might be, but to make His will known to the entire community. The dialogue is always between God and Israel, even though of necessity it is addressed to a specially anointed representative. The same is true in Christianity: the Church is the mystical body of Christ in which all members are joined together. In the Russian branch of Eastern Orthodoxy it is said: "One can be damned alone, but saved only with others" (Smith, 1991, p.354).

The relationship between human beings and God underwent a very significant change from the Judaic to the

Christian tradition. This change, brought about by the influence of Greek thought, is towards an individualizing of the human being's relation to God. This individualizing has its roots in the Psalms and Wisdom Literature, and above all in Jeremiah; but its full implications were not realized until the time of St. Paul (Bultmann, p.223). Many scholars regard this change to be of such fundamental importance that in their view it leads to a radically different type of faith (Buber, 1961, pp.7-12). Significant as these differences are, the fact remains that in the Judæo-Christian tradition in general there is a great deal of emphasis on the community—whether an individual is born into the community, as in the Old Testament, or chooses to belong to one after conversion, so that the whole community is exclusively made up of the converted, as in early Christianity. This community of adherents to a common faith is sustained by the religious injunction to love one's fellow believers.

Faith

As was said earlier, the One who chooses His people is also chosen by them. How do people choose Him? What do they do in return for God's covenant with His chosen people in which He promises to protect them and to lead them? The unequivocal answer, given by the entire Judæo-Christian tradition, can be summed up in a single word: faith. Faith is the wholehearted adherence to the message of the revelations of God, whether it is the Torah, the prophetic utterances, or Jesus Christ himself. Faith is the giving of oneself to be controlled and remade by the one who commands trust and devotion. Faith consists in the total surrender of oneself in the care of God who "neither slumbers nor sleeps." Faith is radical openness to the plenitude of being, characteristically personalized in God whose most sacred and esoteric name is "I AM" (Exodus 3:14). In faith we realize our creatureliness and our guilt and surrender all our "boasting," all desire to live on our own resources. Faith is an unconditional response to the grace of God. It is through faith that we are saved. "Whatsoever is not of faith is sin," says St. Paul in Romans (14:23). The distinctive characteristic of the Biblical religions is not knowledge but faith.

Above all, human beings, the creatures, must realize their nothingness compared to the majesty of God. Although, according to the Biblical story, human beings were created in the image of God, they were soon expelled from the Garden of Eden for their disobedience in the act of eating the forbidden fruit of the tree of knowledge. "And the Lord God said, 'Behold, the man is become as one of us, to know good and evil: and now, lest he put forth his hand, and take also of the tree of life, and eat and live for ever'. Therefore the Lord God sent him forth from the Garden of Eden, to till the ground from whence be was taken. So he drove out the man" (Genesis 3:22-24). The God of judgment punishes all those who disobey Him. Disobedience is a breach of faith, for the primary meaning of faith, both in the Old and the New Testament is obedience. "This is the end of the matter: you have heard it all: Fear God and obey His commands; there is no more to man than this. For God brings everything we do to judgment, and every secret, whether good or bad" (Ecclesiastes 12:13-14).

The Unbridgeable Gap

The lesson that human beings cannot and must not question the ways and motives of God is driven home again and again. We see this in the story of the Tower of Babel (Genesis 11:1-9), and again in the story of Job. The unbridgeable gap between the power and majesty of God on the one hand and the impotence of human beings on the other is strikingly brought out in the Book of Job (Chapters 38-42): God challenges Job to answer, "'Where wast thou when I laid the foundations of the earth, declare, if thou hast understanding... Canst thou lift up thy voice to the clouds, that abundance of waters may cover thee?... Shall he that contendeth with the Almighty instruct him? He that reproveth God, let him answer it...' Job answered the Lord, and said, 'Behold, I am vile, what shall I answer Thee... I know that Thou canst do everything and that no thought can be withholden from Thee. I abhor myself, and repent in dust and ashes.'"

The Old Testament in particular affirms that human beings must know their proper place before God. "The voice said, 'Cry'. And he said, 'What shall I cry? All flesh is grass, and all the goodliness thereof, as the floweres of the field: the grass withereth, the flower fadeth; but the word of our God shall stand forever'" (Isaiah 40:6-8). As Kierkegaard says, "Before God man is always wrong" (quoted by Jung, p. 482). Similar sentiments are expressed in Job (9:1) and Romans (3:20). One of the essential steps on the way to salvation is to recognize and submit to this great gulf between a human being and the Deity. We cannot aspire to become like Him. Indeed to attempt this is the greatest sin of all; this is the very essence of the Devil. This is what Adam was tempted into trying, and he was punished. This is what Lucifer attempted, and he was expelled from heaven. Human beings cannot be saved by their own efforts; salvation comes from outside, by the grace of God to whom, as St. Paul says, one must "pray

without ceasing" (I Thessalonians 5:17). We must fear the
God of redemption, who is *totaliter aliter*, the Wholly Other,
altogether perfect and Outside, the only reality.

> "The Father and I are one."
>
> When some of the Jews again reached for rocks to stone
> him, Jesus protested to them, "Many good deeds have I
> shown you from the Father. For which of these do you
> stone me?"
>
> "It is not for any 'good deed' that we are stoning you,"
> the Jews retorted, "but for blaspheming. You who are
> only a man are making yourself God." (John 10:30-33)

In spite of the teaching and example of Jesus Christ
himself, very few elements of the stream of spirituality that
aims at union or oneness with God have flourished in the
Biblical tradition—a tradition that insists on the unbridgeable
chasm between humans the creatures and God the Creator.
Mysticism of any sort has been suspect but more especially
when it is given a monistic interpretation, that is, when the
soul is said to become one with God. This is particularly
true of the pre-Christian Judaism and the mainstream of
Protestantism which are not only unmystical but definitely
anti-mystical (Zaehner, 1962, p. 171). The creature must never
forget their total dependence on God's grace, which comes
unconditionally when it may. This grace is not a reward for
anything; it cannot be forced or won by any effort
whatsoever. It is a totally undeserved and unearned blessing.
"The highest of human tasks," wrote Kierkegaard, "is for a
man to allow himself to be completely persuaded that he
can of himself do nothing, absolutely nothing"(p. 151).

The Hope for Salvation

"Now faith is the substance of things hoped for, the evidence of things not seen" (Hebrews 11: 1). What is hoped for is redemption from sin and death. If we have faith in the Lord, He will grant us eternal salvation. "God is our refuge and strength," as the psalmist says, "a very present help in trouble" (Psalm 46: 1). "Truly my soul waiteth upon God: from Him cometh my salvation. My soul, wait thou only upon God: for my expectation is from Him. He only is my rock and my salvation: He is my defense, I shall not be moved" (Psalm 62:1, 5-6).

Hope is a dominant note of the Bible, and one of St. Paul's triumvirate of graces (I Corinthians 13:13). In Judaism there was a lively hope that God would deliver the nation from bondage and restore its former glory. This hope fed upon the predictions of salvation in the prophets and lived on in prayers and hymns like the Psalms. Its classical expression is to be found in the apocalyptic literature (Bultmann, p. 94). In its traditional form, the hope of Israel was communal in character. With Jesus, however, it became individual, resting on the eschatological preaching, dealing with redemption and life after death. He believed that a new order was close at hand and the time of decision was in the present. "The time is fulfilled and the reign of God has drawn nigh" (Mark 1:15).

For many Christians the primary religious experience is not faith or love but hope. Their hope is in their own salvation after death and in the Kingdom of God to come in the future. Faith and hope are the dispositions of those who are looking for the grace of God as a future possibility. In this form, they are distinctively Judæo-Christian attitudes. Since one can do nothing on one's own to save oneself, one puts one's faith in the grace of God and hopes for salvation. For this we have the promise of God's prophet:

> Then answered Peter and said unto him, 'Behold we have forsaken all, and followed thee: what shall we have therefore?' and Jesus said unto them, 'Verily I say unto you, that ye which have followed me, in the regeneration when the Son of Man shall sit on the throne of His Glory, ye also shall sit upon twelve thrones, judging the twelve tribes of Israel. And everyone that hath forsaken houses, or brethren, or sisters, or father, or mother, or wife, or children, or lands, for my name's sake, shall receive an hundred-fold, and shall inherit everlasting life'.
> (Matthew 19:27-29)

Hope is what gives us strength in our faith. So does fear of punishment and eternal damnation. Hope and fear are metaphysical and psychological correlates of each other, as are faith and doubt. One invokes the other. One is always afraid that one may not obtain what one hopes for, and that one may not escape the "damnation of hell" to which the unbelievers are doomed (Matthew 23:33). As hope is sustained by God and heaven, so Devil and hell emerge to maintain fear. It is not only faith and hope that are distinctively Judæo-Christian religious attitudes, so are doubt and fear.

Loving Our Neighbours

The third grace in the triumvirate of St. Paul is charity. "And now abideth faith, hope, charity, these three; but the greatest of these is charity" (I Corinthians 13:13). We read in the Bible: "What doth it profit my brethren, though a man say he hath faith, and have not works? Can faith save him?... But wilt thou know, O vain man, that faith without works is dead" (James 2:14, 19-20). While this is characteristic of the New Testament, one would search in vain in the entire Indian tradition for a scriptural passage underscoring the importance of charitable acts for the benefit of the needy and the downtrodden, expressed so forcefully as:

> Then the King will say to those at his right hand, 'Come, O blessed of my Father, inherit the kingdom prepared for you from the foundation of the world; for I was hungry and you gave me food, I was thirsty and you gave me drink, I was a stranger and you welcomed me, I was naked and you clothed me, I was sick and you visited me, I was in prison and you came to me.' Then the righteous will answer him, 'Lord, when did we see thee hungry and feed thee, or thirsty and give thee drink? And when did we see thee a stranger and welcome thee, or naked and clothe thee? And when did we see thee sick or in prison and visit thee?' And the King will answer them, 'Truly, I say to you, as you did it to one of the least of these my brethren, you did it to me'.
>   (Matthew 25:34-40)

Modern translators of the Bible rightly render the Greek *agape*, the third and the highest grace, as love rather than charity, a word which for us moderns has come to mean only benevolent or charitable acts. For St. Paul *agape* is obviously something much greater, as his whole magnificent hymn to love indicates: "And though I bestow all my goods to feed the poor, and though I give my body to be burned, and have not love (*agape*), it profiteth me nothing.... Love never faileth: but whether there be prophecies, they shall fail; whether there be tongues, they shall cease; whether there be knowledge, it shall vanish away" (I Corinthians 13:3, 8).

Above all, God loves human beings. God loved the world so much that He gave His "only begotten son" (John 3:16). To deliver humanity from sin, the Son of God, "who had always been God by nature, did not cling to His prerogative as God's equal, but stripped Himself of all privileges by consenting to be a slave by nature and being born as mortal man. And, having become man, he humbled himself by living a life of utter obedience, even to the extent of dying, and the death He died was the death of a common criminal" (Philippians 2:6-8).

The Son of God died to express His love, for "greater love hath no man than this, that a man lay down his life for his friends" (John 15:13). In return, God demands love for Him and obedience to His laws. "And thou shalt love the Lord thy God with all thy heart and with all thy soul, and with all thy might" (Deuteronomy 6:5). The love of God, which He bestows, and the love of human beings, which He expects, correspond with each other. Sometimes it begins from above: "because the Lord loved you, and because He would keep the oath which He had sworn unto your fathers..." (Deuteronomy 7:8). Sometimes it comes from below: "And now, Israel, what doth the Lord thy God require of thee, but to fear the Lord thy God, to walk in all His ways, and to love Him and to serve Him..." (Deuteronomy 10:12). All else that God requires from the faithful comes from this one thing: because they love Him, they cleave to Him, follow Him in His ways, hearken to His voice, keep His commandments, and serve Him (Deuteronomy 10: 12,13,20; 11: 1, 22; 13:5,18; 19:9). The Lord God wants His people to be holy as He is holy, to be perfect as He is perfect to be merciful as He is merciful (Leviticus 19:2; Matthew 5:48; Luke 6:36).

> 'Master, which is the great commandment in the law?' Jesus said unto him, 'Thou shalt love the Lord thy God with all thy heart and with all thy soul, and with all thy mind. This is the first and the great commandment. And the second is like unto it. Thou shalt love thy neighbour

as thyself. On these two commandments hang all the law
and the prophets'. (Matthew 22:36-40)

Nowhere else in the writings of humanity has loving one's
fellow being been placed so unequivocally on the same level
as loving God; this commandment comprehends all other
ethical precepts. There is no longer any need for formulated
definitions, for we all know how we would like others to
treat us in a similar situation.

Nor is this emphasis on loving one's neighbor an isolated
one in the Judæo- Christian tradition. We read in Leviticus
(19:18): "Thou shalt love thy neighbour as thyself." Hillel, at
the end of the first century BCE, is said to have been the
author of the Golden Rule summary of the Torah: "What is
hateful to thee, do not do to anyone else: this is the whole
law and the rest is commentary." Rabbi Akiba, a century later,
summed up the whole law in the saying: "Love thy neighbour
as thyself." We hear St. Paul saying: "for all the law is fulfilled
in one word, even in this; Thou shalt love thy neighbour as
thyself" (Galatians 5:14). This commandment is so strongly
stated that often it begins to appear to be the centre of the
whole tradition—even foreshadowing the commandment
that precedes it in which we are asked to love God.

The Love of God

Ultimately, however, it is to God that we must return, for
there is no salvation here below, no salvation anywhere or
anyhow except through Him. As long as we live at the level
of our lower nature, the sinful passions work in our bodies
to bear fruit for death. It is only if we repent and turn to God
that our sins can be eradicated (Romans 7:5; Acts 3:19). As

was pointed out earlier, the Greek word which is translated as repentance in the New Testament is *metanoia*; it literally means 'change of mind'. Only if we change our mind and heart and reorient ourselves according to our spiritual nature can we hope for redemption from sin, suffering, and death. "I will tell you this: unless you turn round and become like children, you will never enter the Kingdom of Heaven" (Matthew 18:3). As long as we are by ourselves, depending on our own resources, "bursting with the futile conceit of worldly minds," as St. Paul says, we are in the hands of the evil one (Colossians 2:19). From him we can be delivered only if we put our faith and trust in God, the Holy One of Israel. "We know that so long as we are at home in the body we are exiles from the Lord," and unless we change our heart and repent we shall perish (II Corinthians 5:6; Luke 13:3). But God's grace is lavished upon us when we sincerely seek Him.

> Consider the lilies of the field, how they grow; they neither toil nor spin; yet I tell you, even Solomon in all his glory was not arrayed like one of these. But if God so clothes the grass of the field, which today is alive and tomorrow is thrown into the oven, will he not much more clothe you, O men of little faith? Therefore do not be anxious, saying, 'What shall we eat?' or 'What shall we drink?' or 'What shall we wear... your heavenly Father knows that you need them all. But seek first his kingdom and his righteousness, and all these things shall be yours as well. (Matthew 6:28-33)

Divergence of the Streams

Clearly, each of the two streams is very vast; an immense variety of people, ideas, and practices belong to each. It may even be true that everything that exists in one tradition can be found, in one form or another, in the other. Nevertheless, the mainstreams of the two traditions are very different at the societal, philosophical, and theological level. As one begins to struggle with one's cultural conditioning, it is precisely the mainstream ideas and influences from which one needs to be liberated, so that one is freer to move towards the profounder wellspring of the tradition as well as of oneself. An awareness of another tradition, which does not look at the human situation and possibilities in the same way as our own, can free us for a fresh look at the situation. In the process, we may come to question and understand the very nature of our seeing and of our being. Our seeing may be veiled by conditioning or it may be direct and fresh; our being may be superficial or from the depths.

Though they face the same human condition, the mainstreams of the Biblical and the Indian traditions seem to diverge immensely. The great gulf between the two streams begins right at the beginning—or at least very close to it. Whatever the actual historical beginnings of their sources, the two traditions have acquired very different starting points as far as an individual in the tradition is concerned. Simply put, one begins from the human being and the other begins from God. In India, all spiritual concern centres on the individual person; one finds oneself in bondage or in sorrow, not only as a personal problem but as a mark of a level of consciousness. One struggles to be free of compulsive action (brought about according to the Law of Karma) by a process of self-realization. "I tell you this, the secret of *Brahman*: there is nothing higher than man," declares the *Mahabharata*. (Radhakrishnan and Raju, p.23). There are aids, guideposts, path-markers, teachers, but there are no saviours. "Work out your salvation with diligence," said the Buddha.

In the Biblical tradition, on the other hand, the starting point is God; God is the active agent, who calls human beings to respond to the challenge of His revelation. When we become aware of ourselves, we realize how short we have fallen of what is expected of us by God, how sinful we are. Our awareness of ourselves is through God's revelation. By ourselves, we are nothing; our salvation consists in the recognition of this fact and our total surrender to the will and grace of God, "for by grace are ye saved through faith; and that not of yourselves; it is the gift of God; not of works, lest any man should boast" (Ephesians 2:8-9).

So, St. Paul says, "You...must be obedient...You must work out your own salvation in fear and trembling; for it is God who works in you, inspiring both the will and the deed, for His own chosen purpose" (Philippians 2:12-13).

The Jews and the Christians are very confident of the grace of God to whose protection they can abandon themselves, like children in the care of their mother.

> The Lord is my shepherd; I shall not want.
>
> He maketh me to lie down in green pastures;
>
> He leadeth me beside the still waters.
>
> He restoreth my soul: He leadeth me in the
>   paths of righteousness for his name's sake.
>
> Yea, though I walk through the valley of
>   the shadow of death,
>
> I will fear no evil; for thou art with me,
>
> Thy rod and thy staff they comfort me
>
> Thou preparest a table before me in the presence of
>   mine enemies: thou anointest my head with oil; my
>   cup runneth over.

Surely goodness and mercy will follow me
   all the days of my life;

And I will dwell in the house of the Lord forever.

(Psalm 23:1-6)

In the Indian tradition there are many incarnations (*avataras*) of God, each incarnation corresponding to the requirements of the time and place.   These incarnations can be anthropomorphic or in animal form. In the Biblical tradition, the idea of God being incarnated in animal form is totally abhorrent. Even the idea of human incarnation is quite blasphemous in Judaism and Islam. In Christianity, of course, the single exception is Jesus Christ himself who was "the only begotten son of God" and His equal (John 3: 16; Philippians 2:6). Jesus Christ was declared by the great Church councils to be fully human and fully divine. No one else, however exalted, can be accepted to be divine. Thus, in spite of the many obviously mystical sayings of Jesus, the mainstream of Christianity interprets his message in the manner of the prophetic tradition, with its orientation to God who is essentially different from all others. Human beings are here, God there; He is totally transcendent, both in thought and experience. The prophetic tradition does not accept a continuous scale of being along which there is a vertical movement. Rather, there is a radical discontinuity between animal and human, and more importantly, between human and divine. Any attempt to transcend our humanity towards divinity is a transgression, and is futile and sinful.

In general, the Indian sages seek and find enlightenment within the self, whereas the Biblical prophets are sought by God who reveals His commandments to them. The sacred moments in which the inner core of the human soul communes with the Ultimate Reality are interpreted differently in the two traditions. These may be two radically different experiences, indicating a basic dimorphism in the human psyche. Or, perhaps more likely, these are different interpretations—owing to different languages and cultures—of the same basic encounter. It is possible that at the primary spiritual level the two types of experiences are essentially the same. It should be mentioned that the great Jewish philosopher Philo (30 BCE - 50 CE)—perhaps owing to Greek influence—interpreted the prophetic experience in terms of mystical ecstasy.

In either case, very different concepts of religions and associated terminologies have emerged from this contrast between two kinds of experiences, or two kinds of interpretations of similar experience. In one we have sin, faith, prayer, revelation, grace, and salvation. These are key words in the Judæo-Christian corpus of redemptive literature and form the axis of the whole tradition. All these words sound a little odd in the Hindu-Buddhist context, the hub of which is indicated by other words and ideas: *avidya-maya* (ignorance - illusion), *jñana* (knowledge), *sadhana-yoga* (practice-integration), *samadhi* (meditation-synthesis), *bodhi* (illumination) and *moksha* (liberation).

In the Judæo-Christian tradition the hope of salvation is from outside, from God who is an external absolute and the ultimate authority. Human faith depends on the historical revelation of God through his specially chosen spokesmen. The encounter of an individual with God in the Biblical tradition is mediated, directly or indirectly, by His prophets, by His Word, or by His Church. Any immediate experience is therefore somehow always suspect, for immediacy by its very nature is indifferent to scriptural interpretations, organizational structures, or rational argumentation. These latter tend to constrict reality by insisting that the one true God has expressed Himself through one true Word and one true Church. Hence, in the extreme cases, deviant believers are excommunicated, unacceptable writings are condemned, heretics are burned and heathens are damned. All of these persecutions are a peculiar burden of the history of the Biblical religions. However, this becomes intelligible once we recognize the radical metaphysical dualism, between God and human beings, spirit and flesh, good and evil, which permeates the mainstream of the prophetic tradition. It is this dualism which is ultimately responsible for the dichotomous thinking which has so enthralled Western thought for centuries. There are persistent tensions in Western society: between humanism and theology, between the individual and the cosmos, between the outer world of scientific facts and the inner world of spiritual values, between time and eternity, between this shore and the other. Rarely have these been resolved into a creative synthesis, particularly in the period since the rise of modern science, Protestantism, capitalism, and individualism. Reduced to a single level, these aspects appear to be engaged in a direct either-or combat in which success of one necessarily means defeat of the other.

In the Indian tradition, on the other hand, deliverance is from within, from the innermost core of one's individuality, the core which is the same for all beings. Ultimately, there is no room for a metaphysical dualism here. For the Indians, gods and demons are all inside us, or rather they are us. What one seeks is neither inner nor outer, neither subjective nor objective, neither good nor evil. It is something beyond all these dichotomies and contradictions. There is no external absolute, and the final authority is in the *Atman*, which, although within us, is not the ego-self of human beings. However sacred the writings or any other authority, ultimately it is one's own deepest experience that counts. "When the awakening takes place" says Shankara, "scripture ceases to be authoritative" (commentary on the *Brahma Sutra*, iv.1.3). The risk is that of total relativization and of an indiscriminate acceptance of innumerable gods, sects, and cults; no revelation in space and time is, from this point of view, ultimately any better than another. Thus, at the popular level, mundane history as such, indeed the whole world of space-time, loses significance: after all, it is all a play of *maya*, the cosmic seductress; one must attempt to escape from this enchanting trap, for freedom is not in the world of names and form. Thus for many people in India, truth is regarded to be a personal matter—not only in the sense that it is a subjective experience, but also because it is understood that truth, whatever it may be, must be expressed through a living person. Thus, it becomes important to seek gurus, rather than to seek objective facts about the world or even about oneself.

We must not forget that every tradition has its integrity; it is of a piece. The best insights of the sages and saints of a tradition have a discernible continuity with the worst misunderstandings and perversions of those insights by the mass of the people. This comes about through merciless workings of time, mechanicality, and quantity. The best and the worst of a culture are related to each other, almost as if one cannot exist without the other, except for short times or for small groups of people. The maintenance and continuation of any great truth or vision need such largeness of heart and soul and such sustained self-sacrifice that the general populace cannot live up to it except under strict guidance from the spiritual elite of a community. Common understandings of the great spiritual principles in any religious tradition, precisely because they are common, are unreliable. Mass understandings are only on the surface; they cannot bespeak the depths.

In our attempts to understand the heart of the traditions, we need constantly to return to the experiences and utterances of the sages and saints in the traditions. The essential difference between the two traditions is best brought out in the words of their most illustrious representatives, spoken to their favourite disciples. Christ asked Simon, "Who do you say I am?" He answered, "You are the Messiah, the Son of the Living God." Then Jesus said, "Simon, son of Jonah, you are favoured indeed! You did not learn that from mortal man; it was revealed to you by my heavenly Father. And I say this to you: You are Peter, the Rock; and on this rock I will build my church, and the powers of death shall never conquer it. I will give you the keys of the kingdom of Heaven; what you forbid on earth shall be forbidden in heaven, and what you allow on earth shall be allowed in heaven" (Matthew 16:15-19). The Buddha, on the other hand, said, "Ananda, be ye lamps unto yourselves. Be a refuge to yourselves. Betake yourselves to no external refuge. Hold fast to the truth as a lamp. Hold fast as a refuge to the truth" (Mahaparinibbana Sutta 11.33).

Pilgrim on the Path

On the slopes of the mighty mountain there are many villages, each with its own deity and its own council responsible for the forms of worship and praise for the One who inhabits the mountain top. Every few years, representatives from all the councils gather together to decide which slope is the best for the ascent. They bring evidence and quote authorities, quarrel, and leave. Many move away from the slopes altogether and settle in the plains, some cherishing memories of the stories told by their forefathers after their climb. A few children hear the call from the top, amidst the din of worshippers in the temples and scholars in the councils. Only some of them have the strength and courage to undertake the long and arduous journey leading to the presence of the One who calls.

Who is it that calls us? How can we hear and respond? Is the source of the call inside us or above us? "He who calls you is to be trusted," as St. Paul says (I Thessalonians, 5:24). If we can find a way to trust and attend to this voice, we can leave theorizing aside and begin to learn to respond to the call. If we can keep our central question in mind, we are not likely to distract ourselves by arguments with our neighbours or attempts to convert them. Our need is for some practical way that will help us to be in our *right mind*, by which alone can we hear and see rightly. Until we develop an inner organ of discernment we are without anchor, drifting with any chance wind.

But, each one of us is conditioned by our religious and cultural background, eastern or western. One cannot ignore the remarkable similarities at the primary, experiential level or the profound differences at the secondary, philosophic level between the Judæo-Christian and the Hindu-Buddhist traditions. What one chooses to emphasize depends to a large extent on one's point of view and purpose and on one's social history. In any case, I am convinced that no culture has a monopoly on either stupidity or wisdom. Every culture has had, and will continue to have, great teachers and profound insights.

But it is now more difficult to be parochial than at any other time in the past. In fact, a special sort of imperviousness is required in order to ignore the existence of other great cultures and religions these days. Any one doing so is greatly impoverished, when each one of us might be enriched by becoming heir to the wisdom of all humanity.

In recognition of this fact, individuals and groups have become increasingly interested in fostering interfaith dialogue. The aim of the ecumenical exchanges, which are often regarded as bold initiatives, is to learn about the ideas and practices of other religious traditions. Within the Judæo-Christian context, these initiatives are considered controversial by some and generous by others, because Western traditions are exclusive belief systems.

In a generous comment on my book *The Yoga of the Christ*, the justly highly regarded comparative religionist, Huston Smith, hailed it as a "landmark in interfaith dialogue". However, I have become increasingly uneasy about this comment because I did not wish to engage in interfaith dialogue in that book or in any of my other writings or talks. I have tried to engage in what may be called an interpilgrim dialogue. East-West or interfaith dialogues which are too much bound by the past do not allow the dynamic nature of

cultures and religions—and above all of human beings—
to be appreciated.

If one has never met someone from another culture or
religion, interfaith or intercultural conversation is obviously
a good idea. But I wish to suggest as strongly as I can that
interfaith dialogues are at best a preliminary stage of hu-
man-to-human dialogue and can even be an impediment to a
deeper understanding. A dialogue of cultures and worldviews,
in which the parties involved declare their adherence to one
or another faith or culture, can freeze the way the adherents
talk and think and thus prevent real dialogue. As well,
cultures and religions are continually undergoing large and
serious transformations, if they are alive and dynamic.

An interpilgrim dialogue, which is of necessity somewhat
transcultural, transreligious and transdisciplinary, is needed to
move into a future of a larger comprehension. We don't need
to stunt the growth or prevent a radical reformulation of the
traditions by insisting that everyone declare their adherence
to one or another version of the past. Every major spiritual
teacher, especially the really revolutionary ones like the
Buddha and Krishna and the Christ, has pointed out both the
great call in the subtle core of the traditions and they have
pointed to the betrayal (a word which ironically comes from
the same root as 'tradition') of the real living heart of the
Sacred by these very traditions. To fix the other or myself in
some past mould and thus to deny the possibility of a wholly
unexpected radical transformation is surely a sin against
the Holy Spirit: treating the other as an object rather than a
person, an "it" rather than a "Thou."

These days when I visit my family in the city of
Chandigarh in India, almost everyone I meet has a friend or

a relative who has been to a Western country. Dialogue of worldviews is not merely an academic matter for discussion in learned assemblies. When people brought up in very different cultures, with different religious and musical backgrounds, whisper to each other sweet nothings in intimate embraces, much nonverbal and direct dialogue of worldviews takes place. A great deal of such dialogue is now going on, especially in large urban centers all over the globe.

The products of such dialogues include scholarly cross-cultural and comparative studies of many kinds, as well as literature, films, theater, and music that are not bound by one geographical or national boundary or influence. Above all, an increasing number of children of combined ethnic and cultural parentage, often highly beautiful and intelligent, are by their very existence culture jammers and embodiments of worldviews in dialogue.

Culture is not imbibed only from books. The festivals celebrated in one's family, the music in the background, the myths and legends, the food one eats, and much more, all embody a culture. The musical dialogues between Yehudi Menhuin and Ravi Shankara, and the attempts of Peter Brook to portray the intricacies of the *Mahabharata* in theater are examples of the results of exchanges between cultures. These days, the Governor General of Canada is a woman of Chinese origin; and in 2000, the premier of the Province of British Columbia in Canada was an immigrant from Punjab. In 1999, a Canadian newspaper published a photograph of the CEOs of United Airlines and U.S. Air—two large airlines that were proposing a merger in 1999. Both the CEOs were of Indian origin. All these people are engaged in a dialogue of worldviews, not necessarily under such a label, but in their daily activities. More and more, people from quite different cultural backgrounds are interacting, not necessarily in self-conscious dialogue, but dialogue takes place.

I myself have now lived longer in the Western world than in India. For many years now I have thought and expressed myself in a Western language. Also for years I was trained in physics, which surely has been the Western yoga of knowledge par excellence, and I am married into Christianity and the Western culture. I occasionally ask my friends, or organizers of the symposia to which I am sometimes invited to represent the East, "What makes me an Easterner?" I am happy enough to be an Indian or an Easterner, but what makes me an Easterner? Place of birth? Skin color? Certain philosophical or religious inclinations? Because I am a Hindu I can happily embrace both the Christ and the Buddha, just as anyone can appreciate and love the great creative contributions of Albert Einstein or Dogen Zenzi without having to be a Swiss Jew or Japanese.

I am also the father of children nourished by two great cultures—they are double breeds. They willy-nilly carry on a dialogue of worldviews in their genes. They, and so many of their friends, who are in and out of our home, are more and more transnational and transcultural in their attitudes, tastes, and perspectives. They are not convinced of any need to deny the great wisdom and practices of other religions because of an adherence to the exclusive dogma of a particular religion. They can take delight in and be nourished by not only the two cultures of their parents but even others because they are not wholly hemmed in by the conditioning of one particular culture. Freedom of movement from one position to another and from one language to another

germinates the seeds of delight—a taste of *Brahman*, the
Vastness. A lack of mobility, a sense of being constrained and
constricted, is how Dante conveys the notion of hell. On
the other side, the higher the heaven, the more freedom of
movement; the higher the angels, the more wings they have
so that they can fly with more mobility and felicity.

Juxtaposition without Conquest

One of the outstanding features of our age since the
Second World War is that now a juxtaposition of two major
cultures or worldviews does not necessarily mean that one
of them has to be the victor and the other the vanquished.
This is one of the important features of postmodernism in
the West. The modernist project in the West, dearly beloved
and strenuously pursued during the period from the
European Renaissance to the Holocaust in Nazi Germany and
the atomic incineration in Japan, was predicated on many
assumptions and attitudes. Among these was the assumption—very much supported both by the Western intellectual
tradition and by the major Western religion—that there is
one expression of and one way to truth and that the West has
it, religiously in the form of Christianity and epistemologically
in the form of modern science.

Since World War II, it has been difficult for the Western
intelligentsia to hold this view seriously. It may still energize
mass psychology, but most intellectuals no longer subscribe
to it, certainly not as strongly as they used to.

In liberal scientific circles, it is fashionable now to
acknowledge other ways of knowing; and in liberal Christian
circles the official Church dogma *extra ecclesiam nulla*

salus est (outside the Church there is no salvation) creates various degrees of embarrassment and is often denied and downplayed. Vatican II especially prompted many Roman Catholics to adopt liberal interpretations about the value of other religions, even going so far as to suggest that other religions may lead to salvation. But to the dismay of these Catholics, who cannot quite persuade themselves that the Buddha has less probability of going to heaven than the members of the Mafia, most of whom have been baptized in the Catholic faith, the Vatican periodically swats down such fantasies.

There are several reasons for this massive shift in attitude, some of which are consequences of inherent elements in the two Western institutions mentioned above, namely, science and Christianity. The amazing acceleration and increase in the means of transportation and communication brought about by modern science and technology has resulted in a large number of people from different cultures interacting with people from other cultures—businessmen, students, teachers, volunteers, immigrants, tourists, and scholars.

Christianity has also contributed to the major attitudinal difference, albeit unintentionally. Although very much an Asian religion in its origins, Christianity for the last sixteen hundred years has been associated primarily with Western culture. The conversion of Emperor Constantine in the fourth century made Christianity very much an imperial religion. All the major Christian doctrines were established by the first seven Councils, which were all convened by imperial initiative. The association of Christianity with European centers of power, including colonial power, has continued for so long that a deep Eurocentricism and sense of superiority adhere to Christian dogma and practice.

The conviction that no one can be saved without conversion to Christianity led to an extensive missionary program elsewhere in the world. And the resulting conversions, especially in societies where high birth rates prevail have shifted the religious demographics. Until 1920, more than 80 percent of all Christians in the world were of European descent. Since 1980, however, the majority of Christians in the world are of non-European descent, and a great many of them now live in cultures where they are a religious minority. That fact, coupled with a general decline of European colonialism, has activated a dialogue of world-views. About a decade ago, the World Council of [Christian] Churches was meeting in British Columbia, Canada. A television report on one of their open meetings was a par-ticularly colorful spectacle, much of the color being in the delegates present there from various ethnic groups.

Nevertheless, Eurocentricism and the associated sense of superiority of the European races and culture, which have very much colored Christian doctrine, have not yet been erased by the shift in religious demographics. The late Paulos Mar Gregorios, who was the Metropolitan of the Syrian Orthodox Church in Delhi, told me of an incident that illustrates this fact. Metropolitan Gregorios was a man of much substance: in addition to his religious qualifications, he was a distinguished scholar. At one time he was the President of the Indian Philosophical Congress. He was also for some time the President of the World Council of Churches. In the latter capacity, he had an audience with the present Pope at the Vatican.

In the course of that audience, Metropolitan Gregorios asked the Pope what he thought was the reason for only a small percentage of Indians having converted to Christianity although it had been in India for such a long time. The Pope told him the reason was that the Indian mind was not developed enough to understand the subtlety of thought of St. Gregory of Nyssa or of St. Thomas Aquinas. Somewhat taken aback, Metropolitan Gregorios asked the Pope if he had read Shankara or Nagarjuna. He was immediately shown out of the audience room. I found the incident amusing and not surprising, but Gregorios had been much saddened by it, for the issue was more personal for him. As he said, he realized for the first time that every Indian Christian is considered to be a second-class Christian in the Vatican. This was even more galling for him because he belonged to a branch of Christianity as ancient as any other.

In due course, all this is bound to change. However strongly entrenched, such attitudes hardly represent the best of Christianity. Non-Western cultures of the world have brought forth or fostered quite distinct sorts of Christian understanding. Some people, such as Father Bede Griffiths, have set up Christian ashrams in India, where they have tried to incorporate many distinctly Indian ceremonies and rituals. Many others have learned meditation in the context of Hinduism or Buddhism and have set up Christian ashrams in the West. However, the needed transformations are much deeper than these. What is needed is an interpilgrim dialogue—in which the pilgrims do not already know what God is and what Truth is, but are searching—rather than interfaith dialogues, in which some past councils or texts have already established the creeds and the dogmas one must believe and it does not matter what one's experience actually teaches.

We are—each one of us—on a journey, a journey without end, with a longing for the Infinite. Some of us wish to speak from a pilgrim soul to another pilgrim soul. What is a pilgrim soul? It is a soul that says "not yet", that has a certain restlessness, a willingness to put up with some discomfort, a hunger for the unknown, an inquiry, no fixed positions, a reverence for the journey, a willingness to be surprised. A pilgrim is a student, a searcher, a sojourner here below, a wanderer, not quite satisfied with anything except the Infinite.

Shadows of the Sun

As long as we speak in terms of defined identities as we engage in interfaith or intercultural dialogues, we add to the entrenchment of the "faiths" and "traditions" of the past and interfere with their dynamic transformations, which alone bespeak the life and vitality of the traditions. An illustration of two very subtle insights, one from India and the other from the Biblical tradition, indicate how a nonexperiential dogmatic adherence to past formulations of these insights, possibly their highest insights, have produced shadows.

Indian sages have insisted on the oneness of all there is. This is one of the fundamental truths of the *Sanatana Dharma* (a label for the Indian tradition from the Rig Veda through Gautama Buddha, Mahavira, Nagarjuna, Shankara, Kabir, Nanak, and Ramakrishna to Ramana in our own times). Sometimes this insight is expressed in a stark and transpersonal manner, such as Shankara's realization that all is

Brahman and therefore *Brahman satya jagat mithya*
(*Brahman* is truth, and the world, if seen apart from it, is
false). Sometimes it is expressed in more personal terms,
such as in the Bhagavad Gita, which affirms that all there is,
is Krishna. In spite of differences in the formulations over
several thousand years, the degree to which this essential
truth is realized and embodied marks the largeness of being
and wisdom of a sage.

On the other hand, attachment to an exclusive
traditional formulation of this vision of Oneness has limited
the recognition of the uniqueness of each individual
manifestation. The Indian mind's abstract commitment to the
essential unity of all religions has often prevented a detailed
study and enjoyment of the wondrous and quite remarkably
different manifestations of various religions. Well-meaning
liberal Hindus often claim that Christianity is the same as the
Bhaktimarga or Path of Devotion of Hinduism and that it
leads to the same truth. A practical consequence is that very
few Hindus have ever made a detailed and serious study of
Christianity or of any other religion. There are happy
exceptions, but very few in the long history of the encounter
of India with non-Indian religions.

Can a person, or a religion or a culture, be satisfied and
feel acknowledged, if they are told that they are all essentially
Divine, or lead to Divinity, and that therefore there is no
need to engage with their particularity? An analogy in the
Chandogya Upanishad (6.1.4), much quoted and admired
by the Vedantists, says that clay alone is real, whereas its
modifications are only names arising from speech. However
true this statement may be at the mountain peak of
consciousness—a vantage point achieved by very few

persons in human history—here below it can become a facile and destructive dismissal of all art, uniqueness, and individuality. Is an exquisite Chinese vase the same as a lump of clay?

Turning to the Biblical traditions, we hear the very subtle and powerful enunciation of monotheism in the Jewish Shema: "Hear, O Israel: the Lord our God is one Lord: and thou shalt love the Lord thy God with all thy heart, with all thy soul, and with all thy might" (Deuteronomy 6.4 -5). This proclamation has had an enormous impact on Christianity and Islam as well. Monotheism is often considered by pious people and scholars in the West to be the acme of religious understanding. But no other religious notion has had a more pernicious consequence in creating bigotry and fanaticism than monotheism. Monotheism has resulted everywhere in "My-theism," leading to warfare against other people's religious forms. No one would say, "There is one God, and it is not my God but yours." The late Nobel Laureate Octavio Paz once said:

> We owe to monotheism many marvelous things, from cathedrals to mosques. But we also owe to it hatred and oppression. The roots of the worst sins of Western civilization—the Crusades, colonialism, totalitarianism—can be traced to the monotheistic mindset. . . . For a pagan, it was rather absurd that one people and one faith could monopolize the truth. [Cited by Samuel Huntington, author of *The Clash of Civilizations and the Remaking of World Order*]

Octavio Paz served as Mexican ambassador to India in the 1960s, an experience he regarded as highly significant in both his life and his work, as witnessed by books written during his stay in India, especially *The Monkey Grammarian* and *East Slope*. He could not, therefore, be unmindful of the fact that beautiful sacred buildings are not exclusively related to monotheism—witness the marvelous temples of the "polytheistic" and transtheistic Hindus and Buddhists. Many of these temples were destroyed by the monotheistic fervor that views every other religion's sacred images and buildings with lack of respect or even hatred.

The insistence that the Ultimate cannot be captured in any image or form cannot be sustained by a mind unprepared to live without crutches of form, color, name, beliefs, and dogmas of faith. Every religion has idols; it is only other peoples' idols that monotheists find troublesome, not their own. All scriptures, theologies, and liturgies, no less than images and idols, are particular expressions of religious understandings. Mental idols are more pernicious than idols made of wood or stone because they cannot be so easily seen or seen through. Wilfred Cantwell Smith (with whom I was privileged to teach a course called 'Religions of India' many years ago) has observed, "For Christians to think that Christianity is true, or final, or salvific, is a form of idolatry." And he concludes:

> With a comparative perspective, one sees that "idolatry" is not a notion that clarifies other religious practices or other outlooks than one's own; yet it can indeed clarify with some exactitude one's own religious stance, if one has previously been victim of the misapprehension that the divine is to be fully identified with or within one's own forms. Christians have been wrong in thinking that Hindus are formally idolaters. We would do well, on the other hand, to recognize that we Christians have substantially been idolaters, insofar as we have mistaken for God, or as universally final, the particular forms of Christian life or thought.

> Christianity—for some, Christian theology—has been an
> idol. It has had both the spiritual efficacy of 'idols' in the
> good sense, and serious limitations of idolatry in the
> bad sense.

If we keep hanging on to "faiths" frozen in some past
formulations, we certainly make them into idols in the
pejorative sense of the word. Then it is difficult to see how
one would reconcile the Indian insistence on the oneness of
all there is with the uniqueness of each manifestation, or the
Biblical clarity of knowing that the Ultimate is beyond any
forms whatsoever with the generosity that sees the Divine in
all forms and celebrates image making as an aid to seeing
the Divine.

Interpilgrim exchanges are different by nature. Much
can be exchanged on the mountain slope when one meets
pilgrims coming from different directions and pauses with
them for refreshment and to learn of the dangers on the
journey ahead. Only the actual voyagers on spiritual paths,
the true sages and saints in all the traditions, simultaneously
experience the oneness of all and the uniqueness of each
creature. They stress the ineffability of what they have experienced on the mountain peak while being grateful for all
the images, forms, icons, scriptures, prayers, and rosaries they
used as helpful aids on their journeys.

One may wonder if future pilgrims nourished in the
global culture will still feel constrained to label themselves as
Hindus or Christians. Even if they do, they will be Hindus and
Christians of very different sorts from the ones in the past.
Lest we should think this is all too romantic, we have already
had models of such great beings (*mahatmas*) with large

perspectives: J. Krishnamurti, Sri Aurobindo, Thomas Merton, Father Thomas Berry, Ralph Waldo Emerson, and Henry David Thoreau, to name only a few.

Roaming in many landscapes, physical and cultural, one can gather much insight. As a young man I was a member of the Youth Hostels Association of India. Their motto used to be, and I imagine it still is, *"charan vai madhu vindati,"* "wandering, one gathers honey." I was recently delighted to reencounter this motto in its source, the Aitareya Brahmana (7.15.5).

Looking at the Ganga and Jordan from an Airplane

We can count on, or at least hope, that the religions and faiths which so strongly hold to exclusive formulations will give way to world spirituality and world theology. My writings are occasionally criticized by reviewers who are offended by what they regard to be "spilling Ganges water into the Jordan." It is certainly true that my eyes have been affected by the light reflected from the Ganga. It is also true that the world I live in now and most of the people I encounter have been more influenced by teachings either spoken loudly or whispered on the banks of the Jordan. If the ancient texts are going to have contemporary relevance, both the Ganga and the Jordan will have to be kept simultaneously in view. I could not have arrived where I am now without flying over many rivers, including the Ganga and the Jordan. A view from an airplane surely does reveal different aspects of our planet than does the view from a camel by the Jordan or from a bullock cart by the Ganga.

It surprises me that so many people who are convinced of the universal and objective nature of scientific knowledge work so diligently to find in the latest discoveries of the sciences an exclusive vindication of statements in the Vedas or in the Qur'an or of dogmas accepted by the Church Councils at some stage in history. That we are Hindus or Muslims or Christians largely depends on where we happened to have been born. It is extremely difficult to believe that truth suddenly changes across a border defined by a river or a mountain range corresponding to political boundaries of past or present empires.

I do not have any rigorous data about this, but I imagine that easily 98 percent or even more people in the world sooner or later—especially at the time of marriages or funerals—revert to the ceremonies and the rituals of the religion that they inherited from their forefathers, with minor variations on the theme. This is quite understandable, for, just like ordinary language, much of our emotional-religious language is acquired in early childhood and we make sense of deeper religious aspirations with the aid of these acquired categories of feeling and thought. It is very likely that people who vehemently adhere to one creed or dogma would equally vehemently adhere to another if they had been born in another religious context. The recognition that others exist as thinking, feeling, and autonomous beings who are sometimes engaged with ultimate concerns is a step toward freedom from self-occupation and self-importance, a step of crucial import in spiritual awakening.

Attunement to the spiritual dimension is surely an attunement to a quality of vibration, not exclusively to a particular form of the instrument producing the vibration.

It has not been easy for some to accept that one can have a transfusion of blood from those whose skin color is different from their own. It is much harder to allow the possibility of spiritual nourishment coming from different religious and racial skins. In my own case, I was born a Hindu. There is much that is good and wise in the Hindu tradition. I am certain I could have been dealt a worse heritage. But the Hindus do not have and cannot have a monopoly on Truth or Wisdom or Insight.

One wishes and strives to grow up, part of which is developing a connection with a level of unitive consciousness indicated quite simply by Maharishi Ramana's statement, "There are no others". This does not mean eliminating others in self-occupation, but seeing through the otherness in an integrative perception. It will sadden me if I were merely a Hindu at my death, restricted to my own selfhood defined by contingencies of history or geography. The past is always with us and in us, but future vision needs to be based on some ability to fly with freedom from the past. The more one belongs to God, the less likely one is to belong exclusively to one religion and to claim its monopoly for access to the Ultimate.

> "Sir," answered the woman, "I can see you are a prophet. Our ancestors worshipped on this mountain, but you people claim that Jerusalem is the place where men ought to worship God." Jesus told her, "Believe me, woman, an hour is coming when you will worship the Father neither on this mountain nor in Jerusalem. . . . Yet an hour is coming, and is already here, when those who are real worshippers will worship the Father in Spirit and truth. Indeed, it is just such worshippers the Father seeks. God is Spirit, and those who worship Him must worship in Spirit and truth." (John 4.19-24)

In spiritual matters, what is most relevant is how the quality of a person is affected by whatever theology or philosophy or ritual the person finds helpful. The person—whether oneself or another–cannot be left out of these concerns. Interfaith dialogues are good and possibly helpful, but interpilgrim dialogues are likely to be much more fruitful. We need to be careful not to freeze faiths and the faithful by engaging in "dialogues" that are really simultaneous monologues. Surely the important thing is to see and relate to the person behind the faith. It is not that they are Jews and we are Jains, it is more that some of us have a Jewish background and others of us have a Jain background. At our best, we would wish to be related to the Ultimate or to God, who all our sages say is neither Jewish nor Jain. If we are permanently restricted to relate to each other only as a Jew to a Jain or a Hindu to a Christian, and not as a person to a person, can we ever relate as a person to the Person?

When religions do their job by insisting on the primacy of the person over any system—theological, metaphysical, economic, or political—they are naturally occupied with the cultivation of wise and compassionate people. When such people engage in science, or any other activity, they are naturally concerned for the welfare of all beings, including the earth—not only as generalizations, but also in concrete relationships. As we draw inspiration and instruction from the wise sages and prophets of the past, we will be occupied not only with our personal salvation, but also with the enlightenment of those who will welcome the dawn with song when we are no longer here.

The development of a comprehensive person—one who is closer and closer to the First Person Universal, less as "I am this" or "I am that" and more as "I AM"—is a calling of all religions. The purpose of that development is to awaken from the dead, as St. Paul beautifully said (Ephesians 4.13), to "mature manhood, measured by nothing less than the full stature of Christ."

Dogmatic churches and institutions have, however, a strong hold and much vested interest in preventing a free flow of ideas. My book *The Yoga of the Christ* was published initially in 1990. It was a loving look at the Gospel according to St. John, and somewhat to my surprise it was translated into several languages. In the process of publishing it in Greek, I had such a pitiful request from the Greek publisher in Athens to allow him to change the title, for as he said, "The Orthodox Church will have our publishing house burned down if we published a book with a title containing both 'Yoga' and 'Christ.'"

But there are signs everywhere of pilgrims on spiritual paths, and even that whole cultures are finding something of value in other traditions and cultures—not only because the other is much like us in many ways, but precisely because the other is different from us, a unique manifestation of the Spirit, and can therefore teach us perspectives that have been excluded by our specific cultural conditioning.

With a recognition of the search for truth in each of the traditions and of the way they each express the human situation, we are reminded that the purpose of all spiritual disciplines—which are not the same as religions—is to relate us to the spiritual (which is to say supra-material and supra-mental) dimensions. This tuning into the subtler dimensions is possible only by cleansing our ordinary perceptions and by quieting the mind. The requirement of meditation, as well as of any serious prayer, is to be present with stillness and a silence of the body, mind, and the emotions, so that one might hear a rose petal fall, the sound of the thoughts arising, and the silence between thoughts. The arising of thoughts and emotions is a part of the play of Nature, and watching this play with complete equanimity, without being disturbed, belongs to the Spirit. Alert without agitation, a centered-self without being self-centered, a sage does nothing, nothing of his own or for himself, but everything is accomplished. As Christ said, "I am not myself the source of the words I speak: it is the Father who dwells in me doing His own work" (John 14.10).

The core of all spiritual practice is freedom from the selfish, isolated, and isolating ego so that one can see more and more clearly and be related with all there is more and more lovingly and selflessly. There can be no significance to insight, wisdom, or truth unless it expresses itself in love and compassion. The sages in all the great traditions have said, in myriad ways, that Love is a fundamental quality of the cosmos. Not only a quality but a basic constituent of Ultimate Reality. The Rig Veda (10.129.4) says, "In the beginning arose Love". And the New Testament affirms, "God is love, and he who abides in love abides in God, and God in him" (1 John 4.16). The search for this great Love at the very heart of the cosmos is both the beginning and the end of the spiritual paths, expressed as service, mercy, and compassion—and ultimately as oneness with all other beings. In the very last canto of the *Paradisio* in *The Divine Comedy*, Dante expresses his vision of the highest heaven:

> There my will and desire
> Were one with Love;
> The love that moves
> The sun and the other stars.

The great traditions, in wondrously different ways, have maintained that the Highest Reality—variously labeled "God," "First principle," "Original Mind," "*Brahman*" (literally, "The Vastness"), or simply "That"—is Truth and is Love. In our own days, Mahatma Gandhi maintained, almost like a practical spiritual equation, less to be preached and more to be lived, that God = Truth = Love. The *Theologia Germanica* (chapter 31) says, "As God is simple goodness, inner knowledge, and light, he is at the same time also our will, love, righteousness, and truth, the innermost of all virtues."

The realization of this truth, vouchsafed to the most insightful sages in all lands and cultures, is not something that can be abstracted, bracketed, or packaged. This insight needs to be continually regained, lived, and celebrated. Only when and wherever this realization is made concrete, is there an abundant life of the Spirit. Spiritual disciplines are all concerned with integration and wholeness—above all with the integration of Truth and Love. Love is required to know Truth, and knowledge of Truth is expressed by Love. "The knower of truth loves me ardently," says Krishna in the Bhagavad Gita (7.17), but also, "Only through constant love can I be known and seen as I really am, and entered into" (11.54). A more contemporary remark is by Archimandrite Vasileios of Mount Athos: "For if our truth is not revealed in love, then it is false. And if our love does not flow from the truth, then it is not lasting" (26).

Of course, the search for Love can become merely a personal wish for comfort and security, just as the search for Truth can become largely a technological manipulation of nature in the service of the military or of industry—of fear and greed. Whenever Truth and Love are separated from each other, the result is sentimentality or dry intellectualism in which knowledge is divorced from compassion. Partiality always carries seeds of violence and fear in it. Thus in the name of "our loving God" many people have been killed, just as many destructive weapons have been developed by a commitment to "pure knowledge." But such is not the best of humanity—in science or in religion.

Let Us Not Conclude

Truth in Vastness is beyond all formulations and forms. In being alive to the search, we are alive. Openness to the Sacred always calls for sacrifice, primarily of one's smallness, which is buttressed by an exclusive identification with a particular religion or nation or creed. A person who occupies neither this place nor that—physically or intellectually—may be uneasy, but that is the price of being alive and free.

The only needed realization is that there is a subtle world and that I am seen from that world. My existence now, here, is in the light of the subtler world. To realize the presence of the subtle world and to live in the light of that vision requires a continual impartial revisiting of oneself, which in its turn requires a sacrificing of self-occupation. What is needed is the bringing of the religious mind (which is by definition quiet, compassionate, comprehensive, and innocent) to bear not only on science, but also on technology, arts, government, education, and all other affairs. The religious mind—which is the mind that is suffused with a sense of the Sacred—is cultivated in an individual soul.

This is largely a matter of metaphysical and spiritual transformation, which requires an on-going sacrificing of one's smallness—even more in the heart than in the mind. The new forms will naturally be different. Truth has no history; expressions of Truth do. The new dawn, when we will no longer be there to look at it with the usual eyes, will bring a new song and a new word. But the Essential Word shall abide, often heard in the silence between words.

Integrated human beings in every culture and in every age have searched for both Truth and Love, insight and responsibility, wisdom and compassion. Above the mind, the soul seeks the whole and is thus able to connect with wisdom and compassion. Right order, internally as well as externally, is a movement of energy from the depth to the surface, from above downwards, from Heaven to the Earth. Unless we receive from above, we cannot act for the right maintenance of the world, or as Meister Eckhart put it, "What we receive in contemplation, we give out in love."

Selected Bibliography

Sri Aurobindo. *Last Poems*. Pondicherry: Sri Aurobindo Ashram, 1952.

Collected Poems. Pondicherry: Sri Aurobindo Ashram, 1979.

The Upanishads. Pondicherry: Sri Aurobindo Ashram, 1981.

Buber, Martin. *The Prophetic Faith*. New York: Harper and Row, 1960.

Two Types of Faith. New York: Harper and Row, 1961.

Ten Rungs. Hasidic Sayings. New York: Schocken Press, 1962.

Bultmann, Rudolf. *Primitive Christianity*. London: Collins, 1956.

Coomaraswamy, A. K. *Hinduism and Buddhism*. Brooklyn: Greenwood House, 1971.

Daumal, René. *Mount Analogue*, trans. Roger Shattuck. New York: Penguin Books, 1974.

Dasgupta, S.N. *Hindu Mysticism*. New York: Freidrich Ungar Publications, 1959.

The Dhammapada, trans. I. Babbit. New York: New Directions, 1965.

Durckheim, Karlfried Graf von. *The Way of Transformation: Daily Life as Spiritual Exercise*, London: Mandala Books, Unwin Paperbacks, 1980.

Eliot T. S. *Four Quartets*. London: Faber and Faber, 1996.

Fromm, Erich. *You Shall Be as Gods*. New York: Fawcett, 1977.

Hesse, Herman. *Steppenwolf.* San Francisco: Rinehart Press, 1963.

Humphreys, Christmas. *Exploring Buddhism*. Wheaton, IL: Quest, 1975.

Huntington, Samuel P. In a Los Angeles Times "Global Viewpoint" interview by Nathan Gardels, Oct. 22, 2001.

Huxley, Aldous. *The Perennial Philosophy*. New York: Harper and Row, 1970.

Jung, C. G. "Psychological Commentary on 'The Tibetan Book of the Great Liberation,'" in *Psychology and Religion—West and East*, Bollingen Series XX. Princeton University Press,1958.

Kabir. *One Hundred Poems of Kabir*, trans. Rabindranath Tagore, assisted by Evelyn Underhill, London: Macmillan & Co., 1967.

Kierkegaard, Soren. *Edifying Discourses*. New York: Fontana Books, 1958.

Krishnamurti J. *Commentaries on Living*, 3rd Series, ed. D. Rajagopal. Wheaton, IL: Quest, 1967.

Needleman, Jacob. *The Heart of Philosophy*. New York: Bantam Books, 1982.

   Lost Christianity. New York: Doubleday, 1980.

The New English Bible with the Apocrypha. Oxford University Press and Cambridge University Press, 1970.

Nikhilananda, Swami. *The Gospel of Shri Ramakrishna*. Madras: Mylapore, 1947.

Patañjali. *How to Know God: The Yoga Aphorisms of Patañjali*, trans. Swami Prabhavananda and C. Isherwood. New York: New American Library, 1969.

Prabhavananda, Swami. *The Spiritual Heritage of India*. Hollywood: Vedanta Press, 1979.

Radhakrishnan, S. trans. and ed. *The Principal Upanishads*. Atlantic Highlands, NJ: Humanities Press, 1978.

S. Radhakrishnan and P. T. Raju. eds., *The Concept of Man*. London: George Allen & Unwin, 1966.

Ravindra, Ravi. *The Yoga of the Christ*, Shaftesbury, England: Element Books, 1990. [Re-published as Christ the Yogi, Rochester VT: Inner Traditions International, 1998.]

   Krishnamurti: Two Birds on One Tree, Wheaton IL: Quest Books, 1995.

   Yoga and the Teaching of Krishna, ed. Priscilla Murray, Chennai, India: Theosophical Publishing House, 1998.

Science and the Sacred, Chennai, India: Theosophical Publishing House, 1998 (also Wheaton, IL, Quest, 2002).

Ravindra, R. and Murray, P. "Is the Eternal Everlasting?" in *Yoga and the Teaching of Krishna*, R. Ravindra. Chennai, India: Theosophical Publishing.

Swami Sardananda, *Shri Shri Ramakrishna Lilaprasang*. Calcutta: Udobodhan Office, 1955.

Smith, Huston. *The World's Religions*. San Francisco: Harper, 1991.

Smith, Wilfred Cantwell. "Idolatry in Comparative Perspective." in *The Myth of Christian Uniqueness*, ed. John Hick and Paul F. Knitter, 553-68. Maryknoll, NY: Orbis Books. 1987.

Suzuki, D. T. *Essays in Zen Buddhism*. New York: Grove Press, 1961.

Tagore, Rabindranath. *Gitanjali*. New York: Macmillan, 1971.

Wilson, Colin. *The Outsider*. London: Pan Books, 1963.

Vivekananda, Swami. *The Complete Works of Swami Vivekananda*, Vol. IV. Mayavati: Advaita Ashram Press, 1932.

Zaehner, R. C. *Mysticism—Sacred and Profane*. New York: Oxford University Press, 1961.

The Comparison of Religions. Boston: Beacon Press, 1962.

ed. *The Bhagavad-Gita*. New York: Oxford University Press, 1969.

 Ravi Ravindra was born and received his early education in India before moving to Canada. He was a Member of the Institute of Advanced Study in Princeton in 1977, and a Fellow of the Indian Institute of Advanced Study at Shimla in 1978 and 1998. He was the founding Director of the Threshold Award for Integrative Studies (1978-80), and pilot Professor of Science and Spirituality at the California Institute of Integral Studies in 1989.

At present Dr. Ravindra is Professor Emeritus at Dalhousie University, Halifax, Canada, where he was Professor and Chair of Comparative Religion, Professor of International Development Studies and Adjunct Professor of Physics. Recipient of many fellowships, awards, visiting professorships and research grants, he is the author of more than a hundred and twenty papers in Physics, Philosophy and Religion, and of the following books: *Theory of Seismic Head Waves; Whispers from the Other Shore: Spiritual Search East and West; The Yoga of the Christ* (republished as *Christ the Yogi*); *Krishnamurti: Two Birds on One Tree; Yoga and the Teaching of Krishna; Heart without Measure: Work with Madame de Salzmann*; and *Science and the Sacred*.

In addition to a profound study of the great traditions, Ravi Ravindra has had a longstanding and serious engagement with spiritual search. He has been greatly nourished by his close association with Krishnamurti, with Zen and with the Gurdjieff Work.